John Lang (b. 1816), writer, newspaper editor, traveller and barrister, lived in India for a number of years. A prominent lawyer of his time, he most notably counselled the Ranee of Jhansi in her case against the British East India Company. He was also the editor and publisher of the periodical, *Mofussilite*. Lang's published work includes *The Wetherbys* (1853), *Too Clever by Half* (1853), *Too Much Alike* (1854), *The Forger's Wife* (1855), *Captain Macdonald* (1856), *Will He Marry Her* (1858), *The Ex-Wife* (1858), *My Friend's Wife* (1859), *The Secret Police* (1859) and *Botany Bay; or True Stories of the Early Days of Australia* (1859). John Lang died in Mussoorie in 1864.

In the Court of the Ranee *of* Jhansi
AND OTHER TRAVELS IN INDIA

JOHN LANG

SPEAKING TIGER PUBLISHING PVT. LTD
4381/4 Ansari Road, Daryaganj,
New Delhi–110002, India

Edition copyright © Speaking Tiger 2015

ISBN: 978-93-85288-47-0
eISBN: 978-93-85288-23-4

10 9 8 7 6 5 4 3 2 1

The moral right of the author has been asserted

Typeset in Adobe Jenson Pro by SÜRYA, New Delhi
Printed at Chaman Offset Printers, Delhi

All rights reserved.
No part of this publication may be reproduced,
transmitted, or stored in a retrieval system, in any form or
by any means, electronic, mechanical, photocopying,
recording or otherwise, without the prior
permission of the publisher.

This book is sold subject to the condition that it shall not,
by way of trade or otherwise, be lent, resold, hired out,
or otherwise circulated, without the publisher's
prior consent, in any form of binding or cover
other than that in which it is published.

Contents

In the Court of the Ranee of Jhansi	1
Black and Blue	12
The Mahommedan Mother	34
Tirhoot, Lucknow, Bhitoor, etc	58
The Upper Provinces	78
Marching	98
The March Continued	124
Indian Society	148
Churchyards, etc	171

In the Court of the Ranee of Jhansi

ABOUT A MONTH after the order had gone forth for the annexation of the little province of Jhansi (in 1854), and previous to a wing of the 13th Native Infantry occupying the country, I received a letter in Persian, written upon 'gold paper,' from the Ranee, begging me to pay her a visit. The letter was brought to me by two natives of rank. One had been the financial minister of the late Rajah. The other was the head vakeel (attorney) of the Ranee.

The revenues of Jhansi were some six lacs (60,000*l.*) a year, and after disbursing the expenses of government, and paying the troops in the late Rajah's service, the balance was some two lacs and a half (25,000*l.*) profit. The 'troops' were not numerous, under 1000 in all, and they were chiefly horsemen. The arrangement, when the country was annexed, was simply this: that the Ranee should receive a pension of 6000*l.* a year, to be paid monthly.

The Ranee's object in asking me to visit her at Jhansi was to consult me as to the possibility of getting the order for annexation annulled, or reversed. I should mention that the Ranee had applied to me at the instance of a gentleman of the Civil Service, who had once been the Resident, or Governor-

General's agent, at a native court in the upper provinces; a gentleman who, in common with many other officials of rank in India, regarded the annexation of Jhansi—'a trumpery state after all'—not only as impolitic, but unjust and without excuse. The facts were briefly these:—The late Rajah had no issue by his only wife (the woman who caused our countrymen and countrywomen and children to be put to death in the fort, and who, according to late advices, has been killed), and some weeks previous to his death, being 'sound of mind, though infirm in body,' he publicly adopted an heir, and gave notice to the Government of having done so through the proper channel—namely, the Governor-General's representative then stationed at Jhansi. In short, all the forms required by the Government to prevent fraud in such cases, had been complied with. The child was taken into the Rajah's lap, in the presence of his assembled people, and in the presence of the Governor-General's representative, and he, moreover, signed a document, duly attested, reciting his act and deed. The Rajah was a Brahmin; the adopted boy was a near relative of his.

The Jhansi Rajah had been particularly faithful to the British Government, and Lord William Bentinck had presented the brother of the late Rajah with a British ensign, and a letter giving him the title of 'Rajah,' and assuring him that that title, and the independence attached to it, would be guaranteed by the British Government to him, the Rajah, and his heirs and *successors* (by adoption). That that treaty (for such it purported to be) of Lord William Bentinck was violated, without the slightest shadow of a pretence, there cannot be any sort of doubt. In the time of the Peishwah, the late Rajah of Jhansi was simply a large zemindar (landholder), and had he remained untitled there can be no question that his last wishes, so far as the disposition of his property was concerned, would have been attended to. It was the acceptance of the 'Rajahship' which led to the confiscation of his estates, and the exchange of 6000*l.* a year for 25,000*l.* a year. Strange as that assertion may seem to the reader, it is nevertheless true.

I was at Agra when I received the Ranee's letter, and Agra is two days' journey. Even as I travelled from Jhansi, I sympathized with the woman. The boy whom the Rajah had adopted was only six years old, and during his minority, that is to say, until he had attained his eighteenth year, the Ranee— so the Rajah willed—was to have been the Regent, and the boy's guardian; and it is no small matter for a woman—a native woman of rank, too—to give up such a position and become a pensioner, even on 6000*l.* a year. Let me detail the particulars of my journey to the residence of the Ranee of Jhansi. I got into my palanquin at dusk, and on the following morning, at daylight, arrived at Gwalior. The Rajah of Jhansi had a small house about a mile and a half from the cantonment, which was used as a halting-place, and thither I was taken by the minister and the vakeel who accompanied me. At ten o'clock, after I had breakfasted and smoked my hookah, it was proposed that we 'go on at once.' The day was very warm, but the Ranee had sent a large and comfortable palanquin carriage; in short, it was more like a small room than a carriage, fitted up as it was with every convenience, including even a punkah, which was pulled from the outside by a servant, who sat upon a foot-board. In the carriage, beside myself and the minister and vakeel, was a khansamah, or butler, who, with the apparatus between his knees, kept on cooling water, and wine, and beer, in order that, whenever I felt thirsty, I might be supplied at a moment's notice. This enormous carriage was drawn by a pair of horses of immense strength and swiftness. Each stood about seventeen hands high. The late Rajah had imported them from France at a cost of 1500*l*. The road was rather rough in many places, but, on the average, we got over it at the rate of about nine miles an hour. At about two o'clock in the day we entered the Jhansi territory, having changed horses twice, and we had now some nine miles to drive. Hitherto we had been escorted only by four sowars (horsemen), but now our escort amounted to about fifty, each horseman carrying an immense spear, and dressed much in the same way as the Irregular Cavalry in the pay of the East India Company. And along the road, at intervals of a few hundred yards, were horsemen drawn up, and as we passed, they joined the cavalcade; so that by the time we came in sight of the fortress—if those old weak walls, surmounted by some nine pieces of old ordnance of inferior calibre, deserved the name—the whole strength of the Jhansi cavalry was in attendance. The carriage was driven to a place called 'the Rajah's garden,' where I alighted, and was conducted by the financial minister and the vakeel and other servants of state, to a large tent, which was pitched beneath a clump of gigantic mango trees. The tent, which was that in which the late Rajah used to receive the civil and military officers of the British Government, was elegantly fitted up, and carpeted; and at least a dozen domestic servants were ready to do my bidding. I must not omit to mention that the companions of my journey—the minister and the vakeel—were both men of good ability and pleasing manners. They were, moreover, men of learning, so that my time upon the road had been beguiled very agreeably.

The Ranee had consulted one of the many Brahmins who were supported by her as to the most propitious hour for me to come to the purdah behind which she sat; and the Brahmins had told her that it must be between the setting of the sun and the rising of the moon, which was then near her full; in other words, between half-past five and half-past six o'clock.

This important matter having been communicated to me, I expressed myself perfectly satisfied with the time of the appointment, and ordered dinner accordingly.

This done, the financial minister, after betraying some embarrassment, intimated that he wished to speak to me on a rather delicate subject, and that, with my permission, he would order all the menial servants in attendance on me, including my own sirdar-bearer (valet), to leave the tent and stand at a distance. I complied, of course, and presently found myself alone with only the 'officials' (eight or nine in number) of the little native state of Jhansi. What the finance minister wished to ask me was this—Would I consent to leave my shoes at the door when I entered the Ranee's apartment? I inquired if the Governor-General's agent did so. He replied that the Governor-General's agent had never had an interview with the Ranee; and that the late Rajah had never received any European gentleman in the private apartments of the palace, but in a room set apart for the purpose, or in the tent in which we were conversing. I was in some difficulty, and scarcely knew what to say, for I had a few years previously declined to be presented to the King of Delhi, who insisted on Europeans taking off their shoes when they entered his presence. The idea was repugnant to my mind, and I said as much to the minister of the late Rajah of Jhansi; and I asked him whether he would attend a levée at the palace of the Queen of England, if informed that he must enter her Majesty's presence with his head uncovered, as did all her subjects, from the lowest to the highest. To this question he would not give me a direct answer, but remarked, 'You may wear your hat, Sahib; the Ranee will not mind that. On the contrary, she will regard it as an additional mark of respect towards her.' Now this was what I did not want. My desire was, that she should consider the wearing of my hat, supposing I consented to take off my shoes, as a species of compromise on her part as well as on my part. But I was so amused with this bargaining, as it were, that I consented; giving them distinctly to understand, however, that it was to be considered not as a compliment to her rank and dignity, but to her sex, and her sex alone. That great point settled, I partook of a very sumptuous repast that was prepared for me, and awaited patiently the setting of the sun or the rising of the moon, determined, however, that I would wear my hat—a black 'wide-awake,' covered with a white turban.

The hour came, and the white elephant (an Albino, one of the very few in all India), bearing on his immense back a silver houdah, trimmed with red velvet, was brought to the tent. I ascended the steps, which were also covered with red velvet, and took my place. The mahoot, or elephant-driver, was attired in the most gorgeous manner. The ministers of state, mounted on white Arabs, rode on either side of the elephant; the Jhansi cavalry lining the road to the palace, and thus forming an avenue. The palace was about half a mile distant from my encampment ground.

Ere long we arrived at the gates, at which the attendants on foot began to knock violently. A wicket was opened, and closed hastily. Information was then sent to the Ranee; and, after a delay of about ten minutes, the 'hookum' (order) came to open the gates. I entered on the elephant, and alighted in a court-yard. The evening was very warm, and I fancied that I should be suffocated by the crowd of natives (retainers) who flocked around me. Observing my discomfiture, the minister imperiously commanded them to 'stand back!' After another brief delay, I was asked to ascend a very narrow stone staircase, and on the landing was met by a native gentleman, who was some relative to the Ranee. He showed me first into one room and then into another. These rooms (six or seven), like all rooms of the kind, were unfurnished, save and except that the floors were carpeted; but from the ceiling punkahs and chandeliers were suspended, and on the walls were native pictures of Hindoo gods and goddesses, with here and there a large mirror. At length I was led to the door of a room, at which the native gentleman knocked. A female voice from within inquired, 'Who is there?'

'Sahib,' was the reply. After another brief delay, the door

was opened by some unseen hand, and the native gentleman asked me to enter, informing me, at the same time, that he was about to leave me. A brief delay now occurred upon my part. It was with great difficulty that I could bring myself to take off my shoes. At length, however, I accomplished it, and entered the apartment in 'stocking feet.' In the centre of the room, which was richly carpeted, was an arm-chair of European manufacture, and around it were strewn garlands of flowers (Jhansi is famous for its beautiful and sweet-smelling flowers). At the end of the room was a purdah or curtain, and behind it people were talking. I sat myself down in the arm-chair, and instinctively took off my hat; but recollecting my resolve, I replaced it, and rather firmly—pulling it well down, so as completely to conceal my forehead. It was a foolish resolve, perhaps, on my part, for the hat kept the breeze of the punkah from cooling my temples.

I could hear female voices prevailing upon a child to 'go to the Sahib,' and could hear the child objecting to do so. Eventually, he was 'launched' into the room; and upon my speaking kindly to the child, he approached me—but very timidly. His dress and the jewels on his person, satisfied me that the child was the adopted son of the late Rajah, and the rejected heir to the little throne of Jhansi. He was rather a pretty child, but very short for his years, and broad-shouldered—like most of the Mahratta children that I have seen.

Whilst I was speaking to the child, a shrill and discordant voice issued from behind the purdah, and I was informed that the boy was the Maharajah, who had just been despoiled of his rights by the Governor-General of India. I fancied that the voice was that of some very old woman—some slave or enthusiastic retainer, perhaps; but the child having imagined that he was spoken to, replied, 'Maharanee!' and thus I was told the error of my conclusion.

And now the Ranee, having invited me to come closer to the purdah, began to pour forth her grievances; and, whenever she paused, the women by whom she was surrounded, set up a sort of chorus—a series of melancholy ejaculations—such as 'Woe is me!' 'What oppression!' It reminded me somewhat of a scene in a Greek tragedy—comical as was the situation.

I had heard from the vakeel that the Ranee was a very handsome woman, of about six or seven and twenty years of age, and I was very curious indeed to get a glimpse of her; and whether it was by accident, or by design on the Ranee's part, I know not, my curiosity was gratified. The curtain was drawn aside by the little boy, and I had a good view of the lady. It was only for a moment, it is true; still I saw her sufficiently to be able to describe her. She was a woman of about the middle size—rather stout, but not too stout. Her face must have been very handsome when she was younger, and even now it had many charms—though, according to my idea of beauty, it was too round. The expression also was very good, and very intelligent. The eyes were particularly fine, and the nose very delicately shaped. She was not very fair, though she was far from black. She had no ornaments, strange to say, upon her person, except a pair of gold earrings. Her dress was a plain white muslin, so fine in texture, and drawn about her in such a way, and so tightly, that the outline of her figure was plainly discernible—and a remarkably fine figure she had. What spoilt her was her voice, which was something between a whine and a croak. When the purdah was drawn aside, she was, or affected to be, very much annoyed; but presently she laughed, and good-humouredly expressed a hope that a sight of her had not lessened my sympathy with her sufferings nor prejudiced her cause.

'On the contrary,' I replied, 'if the Governor-General could only be as fortunate as I have been, and for even so brief a while, I feel quite sure that he would at once give Jhansi back again to be ruled over by its beautiful Queen.'

She repaid this compliment, and the next ten minutes were devoted to an interchange of such matters. I told her that the whole world resounded with the praises of her beauty and the greatness of her intellect; and she told me that there was not a corner of the earth in which prayers for my welfare remained unsaid.

We then returned to the point—her 'case.' I informed her that the Governor-General had no power to restore the country, and recognise the claim of the adopted son, without a reference to England, and that the most prudent course for her to adopt would be to petition the throne, and meanwhile draw the pension of 6000*l.* a year, under protest that it was not to prejudice the right of the adopted son. At first she refused to do this, and rather energetically exclaimed: 'Mera Jhansi nahin dengee' (I will not give up my Jhansi). I then pointed out to her, as delicately as possible, how futile would be any opposition; and told her, what was the truth, that a wing of a native regiment and some artillery were within three marches of the palace; and I further impressed upon her that the slightest opposition to its advance would destroy her every hope, and, in short, jeopardize her liberty. I did this because she gave me to understand—and so did her attorney (and my impression is that they spoke the truth)—that the *people* of Jhansi did not wish to be handed over to the East India Company's rule.

It was past two o'clock that night before I left the palace; and ere I took my departure, I had talked the lady into my way of thinking, except that she would not consent to draw any pension from the British Government.

On the following day I returned to Gwalior, *en route* to Agra. The Ranee presented me with an elephant, a camel, an Arab, a pair of greyhounds of great swiftness, a quantity of silks and stuffs (the production of Jhansi), and a pair of Indian shawls. I accepted these things with great reluctance, but the financial minister entreated me to take them, insomuch as it would wound the Ranee's feelings if I refused. The Ranee also presented me with a portrait of herself, taken by a native, a Hindoo.

The state of Jhansi was not restored to the rule of the Ranee, and we know that she afterwards rivalled that fiend Nena Sahib, whose 'grievance' was identical with her own. The Government would not recognise Nena Sahib as the adopted son and heir of the Peishwah; the Ranee of Jhansi sought to be recognised as the Regent during the minority of the late Rajah's adopted son and heir.

Black and Blue

FORTY YEARS AGO there went out to India, in the good ship *Globe*, Ensign the Honourable Francis Gay, a younger son of the Right Honourable the Earl of Millflower. The ensign was in his nineteenth year, and was proceeding to join his regiment, which was stationed at Chinsurah.

Lord Millflower, in his heart, hoped that his son would never return: he was so great a disgrace to his family. There was no vice with which this youth was unfamiliar. He had been expelled from no fewer than seven schools. In two instances his offence was theft. His conduct had so preyed upon the mind of Lady Millflower that she lost her reason. At seventeen, he committed several forgeries of his eldest brother's, Lord Larkspeare's name; and he took a similar liberty with the name of his father's steward. But these offences were hushed up. He was also guilty of a deed of violence, for which his life would have been forfeited had the case been tried, instead of compromised; for in those days such a deed of violence was a capital offence. His family were in constant fear lest he should be transported as a felon, or hanged at Newgate. It was, therefore, some satisfaction to them when the Honourable Francis consented to hold a commission and join his regiment in India. Lord Millflower's other sons, four in number, were all steady, well-conducted, and rather dull beings, while Francis was remarkably gifted, as well as remarkably vicious. He had both talent and genius, humour and wit; and, much as he had neglected his education, he was well read and well informed for his time of life. In personal appearance, also, the reprobate had the advantage over his brethren. None of them were even good-looking except Francis, who was really very handsome, well proportioned, and tall. His manners also, always frank, were, when he pleased, dignified and courteous, and his bearing peculiarly graceful. What he wanted was feeling, to regulate his passions. Of feeling, he was in his youth, wholly destitute.

Lord Millflower had taken the precaution of writing to the colonel of the regiment his son was about to join, and of at the same time enclosing a sum of money for the purpose of freeing Francis from any pecuniary difficulty. Colonel Role himself had the misfortune to have a very bad boy, and he, therefore, sympathized deeply with the worthy nobleman, and resolved to do all in his power to reform the Honourable Francis.

After a passage of four months, the *Globe* arrived at Calcutta, and the Honourable Francis Gay proceeded to Chinsurah and joined. For several weeks he conducted himself with (for him) wonderful propriety. It is true, that he drank and played at billiards and cards, and sometimes an oath would escape his lips, but he indulged in no excesses. The officers of the regiment, indeed, thought the ensign a great acquisition, for he was not only a very pleasant but an entertaining companion.

But, by degrees, the Honourable Francis fell off; and ere long, so far from having a friend in the regiment, there was no one who would speak to him. Even the colonel was compelled to forbid him his house. Many, very many acts, unbecoming the character of an officer and a gentleman, had been looked over by his seniors; but it was resolved that, on the very next occasion of his transgressing, the Honourable Ensign should be brought to a court-martial and dismissed from the service. This resolve was communicated to the ensign by the colonel, who had become tired of lecturing him.

'The next time you are intoxicated on the parade ground, or the next time you use bad language in the mess-room, or the next time you publicly insult a brother officer, provoking him to quarrel with you, you will forfeit your commission.' Being the son of an earl, he was entitled—many colonels think—to every possible chance of redemption. Had he been the son of a commoner, he would, most probably, have been court-martialled and cashiered for the very first offence.

'Thank you, sir,' replied the ensign, with a low bow; 'I will be more cautious in future.'

He kept his word. From this time he did his duty extremely well; and, to all outward appearance, was a reformed character. The officers observing this, generously made advances with a view to resuming their former relations with him. But the Honourable Francis repulsed their advances. The whole regiment had thought proper to cut him; and he now thought proper to cut the whole regiment.

Several months passed, and during that period the ensign applied himself to Hindostanee and Persian. He encouraged the natives to come to his bungalow, to talk with him, and by night and by day pursued his studies. The result was, that he soon conversed with perfect ease and accuracy. He now began to live like a native—a Mahommedan; and, except when he had to attend to his regimental duties, he wore the native costume, and abstained from drink entirely. With truth, he might have said with Conrad,—

> The grape's gay juice my bosom never cheers;
> I'm more than Moslem when the cup appears.

His food was rice, milk, vegetables, and fruit; the bed upon which he slept was hard and mean; such as the natives use. The whole of his European furniture he sold by auction.

His desire—the desire of a doubtfully reformed reprobate—to convert to Christianity a young Mahommedan girl, astonished all those who became acquainted with this desire. The girl was the daughter of a water-carrier (Bheestie). She was not like the natives of India, but more like those of Africa. She was coal black, and had thick lips and wavy hair. She was short for her age—fourteen years—but thickset, with powerful limbs. The girl's father told the servants belonging to other officers of the regiment, and the curious whim of Gay's became a topic of conversation.

Jehan, the bheestie's daughter, was a virtuous girl, and Francis Gay had never approached her with a view to undermining her virtue. It was no easy matter to persuade her to change her religion; but, strange to say, he at length succeeded, and Noor Jehan was baptized as Ellen by a missionary who journeyed to Chinsurah for the purpose of performing the ceremony. The sanity or otherwise of the ensign was now very generally discussed in the regiment, and the prevalent opinion was that he was a lunatic. But the good colonel was a little angry at the surmise. 'Surely,' he said, 'you do not accuse a man of being a maniac because he has converted an infidel.'

The regiment was ordered to march to Cawnpore, whither Ellen and her father also proceeded. Cawnpore was then the chief station in the upper provinces of India. Five thousand troops were quartered there. A regiment of dragoons, a regiment of native cavalry, a regiment of British infantry, and two of native infantry. Besides horse and foot there were companies of artillery, and sappers and miners.

Very shortly after the regiment was settled in Cawnpore, the Honourable Francis Gay paid a visit to the chaplain, and intimated a desire to be married. The chaplain of course replied that he should be most happy, and there and then a day and hour was appointed for the performance of the rite; but, when the reverend gentleman came to hear who was to be the Honourable Ensign's bride—the black daughter of a native water-carrier—he could not help remarking:

'I am sorry, Mr. Gay, that I cannot with sincerity offer you my congratulations.'

To which the ensign responded:

'My good sir, I did not ask them.' And retired with a bow.

The chaplain drove to the house of Colonel Role, and told him of the interview which had just taken place between himself and Ensign the Honourable Francis Gay. The colonel called upon the young man, and entreated him to reflect. 'I *have* reflected, sir,' was the ensign's reply. The colonel then went to the general, and the general sent for Mr. Gay to attend at his bungalow. Mr. Gay obeyed the summons, and listened with attention and much calmness to a long and violent speech. When it was ended, however, Mr. Gay, with extreme courtesy, and in the quietest of tones, spoke thus:

'General, you had a right to command my attendance here upon any military matter, but not upon any civil matter. However, I waive that, because I believe your intention to be a good one. You, general, have arrived at the years of discretion—perhaps at something beyond those years. You have, at all events, arrived at a time of life when the tumultuous passion of youth can no longer be pleaded in extenuation of certain follies. Now tell me, general, which of us, think you, sins the most, and sets the worst example to the men, European and native, in this station?—I, who wish to marry this good Christian girl; or you, who have in your house—' Mr. Gay then made mention of two very discreditable members of the general's establishment. 'This is a question which I shall put to the commander-in-chief, if you abide by your threat to report me to his excellency.'

That night the general and Colonel Role held a consultation. The colonel still doubted the ensign's insanity. It had become a fixed idea in the regiment that Gay was insane. The general caught at this, and a committee of doctors was appointed to examine the ensign. They reported that Ensign the Honourable Francis Gay was not only of sound mind, but one of the most intellectual young men in the station; and that he had explained to their entire satisfaction certain conversations which he had frequently held with himself in Chinsurah, at the mess-table.

The wedding-day had been put off in consequence of these proceedings; but the parties now met in the church, which was crowded with officers, including nearly the entire medical staff, who were curious to witness the spectacle. There stood the tall and handsome English aristocrat, and beside him his coal-black bride, dressed in garments of red silk, trimmed with yellow and gold tinsel. The ensign acted as the interpreter, and explained to Ellen in Hindoostanee the vows she was required to take. This made the ceremony a very long one. When it was concluded, the bride got into her palanquin and was carried home. The bridegroom mounted his pony, and rode by her side.

Ellen—now the Honourable Mrs. Gay—was a girl of great natural ability, of an excellent disposition, and was blessed with an excellent temper. She had, moreover, a very sweet voice. After her marriage she was never seen by any European in Cawnpore, except her husband. It was believed that the ensign saved more than two-thirds of his pay, which Ellen, who had an excellent idea of business, used to lend out in small sums to people in the bazaar at the rate of fifty per cent. per mensem. If she lent a rupee (two shillings), she would get back at the end of the month a rupee and eight annas (three shillings) by way of interest.

A year passed away, and a son and heir was born to the Honourable Francis Gay. The child had light blue eyes, exactly like those of his father; but his complexion was quite as black as his mother's. When the child was three months old, it was brought to the church, and publicly christened, Mr. Gay and the pay-sergeant of the company he belonged to being the godfathers, and Ellen the godmother. The names given to the infant were Ernest Augustus George Francis Frederick—such being the names respectively of Lord Millflower's sons. Ernest was the eldest, Augustus the second, George the third, Francis the fourth, and Frederick the fifth and youngest. Not long after the birth of his son, Ensign Gay obtained his promotion to the rank of lieutenant, and received, of course, an increase of pay.

Fever became prevalent, and cholera. Several of the captains and senior lieutenants fell victims; and, in less than three years, Lieutenant Gay got his company (the regiment was now at Meerut), and retired from the army by the sale of his captain's commission. It was supposed that he was worth a great deal of money—a lac of rupees (ten thousand pounds) at the very least. Whither he went no one knew, and no one cared. One of the servants, whom he discharged previous to leaving the station of Meerut, said he believed that his master had gone either to Affghanistan or to Lahore.

Let us now return to Europe. A few years after Captain Gay had sold out of the army, his eldest brother, Lord Larkspeare, was killed while grouse-shooting, by the accidental discharge of his gun; his second brother, Augustus, a captain in the army, was lost in a vessel which was bringing him home from Canada; his third brother, George, died of small-pox three days after he had taken his father's second title. Of his son Francis's marriage, Lord Millflower had been informed, and also of the birth of the black child, the

Honourable Ernest Augustus George Francis Frederick Gay. Colonel Role had deemed it his duty not to withhold these facts, albeit they were disagreeable to communicate to the noble earl. Lord Millflower begged of Colonel Role to institute an inquiry into the fate of his Francis, and the Colonel did so, but without success. No clue to his whereabouts could be discovered, nor could any one say what had become of him. Under these circumstances it was taken for granted that he was dead. Another five years passed away, and the Earl of Millflower departed this life. He was, of course, succeeded in his titles and estates by his son Frederick.

Now let us return to Francis. He became a dealer in precious stones, and travelled over the whole of India, under the name of Mustapha Khan, visiting the various native courts. Every tour that he made occupied him three years. Constantly moving about in the sun had tanned his once fair face; and neither from his appearance—for he was dressed as a native—nor from his speech, could the natives themselves detect that he was an European. He gave out that his birthplace was Nepal, where the natives are sometimes born with blue eyes. He bought and sold, and was apparently very happy in his occupation.

His wife and son invariably accompanied him in his travels. He had never written to his family since his arrival in India, and had not received letters from any member thereof. India he loved, England he detested, and would not have taken up his father's title if it had been a dukedom. He never approached the abode of an European, and never saw a newspaper. He was not likely, therefore, to hear of the changes that had taken place at home. In the bazaar at Delhi Captain Gay had a small house, in which were deposited his effects, a few boxes filled with clothes, books, &c., his sword, and the uniform he used formerly to wear. These were under the care of a man-servant, a sweeper. The bulk of his worldly wealth he invariably carried about his person, as many natives of India do.

Ernest Gay was now twelve years of age. He was usually called by his parents Chandee, a word signifying silver. Chandee was clever and cunning, and had a wonderful talent for calculating numbers. In less than a minute, by counting on his fingers, he would tell you the interest due on such sums as three rupees, five annas, and seven pic, for twenty-one days, at forty-one three-fourth per cent. English he had never heard spoken; and as he had never been taught that language, he did not understand a single word of it. Nor could he read or write Hindoostanee, although he spoke it in all its purity and elegance.

There was about to take place a marriage in the family of the Rajah of Pulbecala. Mustapha Khan (Francis Gay) journeyed from Delhi to the Rajah's court, to exhibit his jewels. He had diamonds, rubies, and emeralds of great price, and some of these he hoped to dispose of to advantage. The Rajah, however, had already provided himself with these matters, and therefore confined his purchases to a large cat's-eye ring, for which he paid Mustapha fifty gold mohurs (eighty pounds). On his way back to Delhi, at a place called Kunda Ka Serai, a band of robbers attacked the jewel-merchant. They hacked him to pieces with their swords, but they spared his wife and the boy. The whole of their treasures were stolen; even the rings from Ellen's ears and fingers, and the gold bangles which Chandee wore upon his arms.

When her senses were restored to her, Ellen, with the assistance of her son, dug a grave in the sand, and buried her butchered husband. The bearers who carried the palanquins ran away as soon as the robbers attacked the party, and were no more seen. Most probably they had some small share of the booty, the value of which the Sirdar estimated at four lacs of rupees (forty thousand pounds). Whatever had been Francis Gay's vices when a youth—and they were great enough in all conscience—he had been a kind and affectionate husband to Ellen, and she most bitterly deplored his loss; violent was the grief of Chandee, who was devotedly fond of his father.

They heaped stones over the grave of the dead man, to mark the spot where he was laid, and, after their own fashion, offered up prayers for the repose of his soul.

The murder having been committed within the dominions of an independent prince, Ellen knew that her wrongs were not likely to be redressed if she complained; and that the British Government would not interfere, unless she made known that her husband was an Englishman. This she felt would be contrary to the wishes of the dead. Hopeless and helpless, she and her son made the best of their way to Delhi, where, having collected a few debts that were due to them, they established a small shop for the sale of native sweetmeats. They carried on this business for three or four years, when Chandee grew weary of it, and set up in the world as a box-waller, or pedler. His box contained pens, ink, and paper, needles, pins, knives, scissors, soap, eau de Cologne, toothbrushes, matches, and so forth. His customers were the European officers, who gave him the name of Black and Blue, from the colour of his eyes and skin. A box-waller is always a great cheat—as great a rascal as was Autolycus himself; Black and Blue, if the truth must be told, was not an exception to the rule or race. But no one could grudge him his profits when the cuffs and kicks which were playfully administered to him by the young lieutenants and ensigns are taken into consideration. Black and Blue always took the rough usage of his customers in excellent part; and would generally make some such appeal as this (he had picked up a little English by this time): 'Ah, well! I know! You rich white gentlemans—I poor black devil. I pray all day all night that ensign be made leeft'nunt; leeft'nunt, capitaine; capitaine, capitain-meejor; meejor, kunnull; kunnull, meejor-jinneral; and then God bless your father and mother, and brother and sister; and then, for all that pray, I get so much kick and so many bad words. God make us all—black and white; all equal right up above. You want blacking? Here you are. Very good blacking—quite genuine; only one rupee a bottle. I suppose you not got ready money! Very well, I wait till pay-day come. I very poor man. You my master. Khuda Lord Kuren.' The meaning of this expression, with which most natives wind up a speech to an European, signifies, May God make you a lord!

When Black and Blue was no more than five years old, he was playing one morning in his father's compound (enclosure—the land around the bungalow), when a pariah dog rushed in and mangled him very severely. The dog was rabid. Captain Gay called in the doctor of a native cavalry regiment, who lived in the next bungalow, who cauterized the wounds. The child was bitten on the arms, legs, and chest, and was under the doctor's treatment for upwards of five weeks. On several occasions when he visited his patient, the doctor saw and conversed with Ellen, who was naturally very anxious touching the child's safety. This doctor was one of the number who witnessed the marriage of Ensign Gay at Cawnpore, and was also present when his offspring was christened.

Shortly after the recovery of the little boy, the doctor had been appointed a presidency surgeon, and had charge of one of the hospitals in Calcutta, where he remained for upwards of twenty years. He was then appointed superintending surgeon of the Meerut division. He had a son at Delhi, a lieutenant in the foot artillery, and occasionally went over (the distance is only forty miles from Meerut) to pay him a visit.

On one of these occasions, Black and Blue, who had been sent for, made his appearance with his box, sat down on the carpet cross-legged, and opened out his treasures. There were several young officers in the bungalow, chums of the lieutenant; and, while the bargaining was going on, they began to tease Black and Blue. One removed his turban with the point of a stick; another sprinkled him with his eau de Cologne; a third touched the tip of his great toe (he had left his shoes, out of respect, in the verandah) with the lighted end of a cheroot. Black and Blue howled with pain, whereupon the two roared with laughter. The doctor, who was reading a paper, begged the young men to desist, and, somewhat angrily, expostulated with his son for treating a native so cruelly; for he was touched with poor Black and Blue's appeal—'God make us all. When fire burns black man, black man feels as much pain as white man. In hell, you rich gentlemans sing out just as much as poor box-waller.'

'Black and Blue is used to it, governor,' said the lieutenant.

'Stuff, Robert!' said the doctor; 'I address myself to you, and not to these gentlemen, when I say that I have no patience with such flippant cruelty.'

'Sahib,' said Black and Blue, looking up at the doctor, 'you are very good gentlemans—very kind man, and very handsome. May God make you a lord; may your throne be perpetual, and may your end be peace; but do not be angry with these gentlemen. They play tricks with Black and Blue; but they are no enemies. If enemies, what for send to buy Black and Blue's property? Sir, you greatly oblige Black and Blue if you smile once more on these gentlemans. Sir, do you want any violent (violet) powder, or one small patent corkiscrew (corkscrew)? All men born equal; God's rain wet black man and white man all the same. Devil's fire burn, too, both the same.' Here he laughed at the lieutenant. 'Take one packet of violent-powder. Every one rupee a packet. Well, then, take two for one, twelve. That can't hurt anybody. Less than prime cost, I give you my solemn word. Handsome sir, don't be angry.'

The doctor, his attention attracted by those light blue

eyes, set in that very black skin, stared at Black and Blue for several minutes after he had finished the speech above quoted. He had never before seen such a peculiar expression as that on the face of the box-waller. Suddenly he recollected an instance of black skin and light blue eyes; but in that case the boy was half-European, the child of the Honourable Francis Gay.

Black and Blue had occasion to change his position; and, in doing so, exposed the calves of his legs. On one of them was a scar, quite round, and about the size of a shilling.

'Good God!' exclaimed the doctor, who became both surprised and agitated, and allowed the newspaper to fall from his hand.

'What is the matter, governor?' asked the lieutenant.

'Nothing—nothing!' said the doctor, still staring at Black and Blue, whose countenance was no longer strange to him. 'How did you come by that mark?' he at length asked, pointing to the scar.

'I don't know, Sahib.'

'But did not your parents ever tell you?'

'No, Sahib. Parents used to say that it come of itself.'

This was no doubt true.

'Have you another mark like that on your right arm—just here?'

The doctor placed his finger on the sleeve of the man's dress.

'Yes. But bigger mark that one. How you know that, Sahib?' He pulled up his sleeve and exhibited a scar the size of half-a-crown.

'And another here—on your hip—and another here, on your ribs?'

'Yes. All them marks got, sir. How you know that, Sahib?'

The doctor was quite satisfied that Black and Blue was no other than his little patient of former years, and consequently the heir to the Earldom of Millflower. Could it be possible, he thought, that Captain Gay eventually abandoned his black wife and child! If not, how came it that the boy (now a man of two or three and twenty) should be a miserable pedler, living in the Bazaar at Delhi? When Black and Blue had sold all that the young officers wanted to buy—when no amount of coaxing and flattering would induce them to take anything more—he was about to take his departure; but the doctor desired him to stay, and intimated to his son that he wished to have some conversation in private with Black and Blue.

'Where is your father?' the doctor asked.

'He dead, Sahib.'

'When did he die?'

'Long time ago—ten or twelve year ago.'

'Where did he die?'

'Mans—robber mans—kill him with sword.'

'And your mother?'

Black and Blue told the doctor the whole of their history since the death of Captain Gay, and his statements were substantially true. Black and Blue, however, declared most positively that his father was a native, and no European.

'Do you think,' the doctor inquired, 'that your mother would see me, if I went down to her home?'

'O yes—why not? Come along, Sahib. I will show where she live. You call for palanquin and get on. I run alongside.'

The doctor's curiosity was very strong, and he could not resist the desire to satisfy it at once. He accepted Black and Blue's invitation, and went to the house occupied by Ellen. Habited as a native, she was sitting on a coarse mat, smoking, and at the same time mending an old garment of her son's.

The doctor recognised Ellen immediately, albeit she was now aged. But at first she did not recognise him. He was altered very much in appearance. His hair and whiskers had become very grey, and he no longer wore a moustache.

Ellen parried all the questions that were put to her, and affected to be as much surprised by them as by the doctor's visit. The statement of her son she supported, that her husband was a native of India.

'O, but surely,' said the doctor, 'this was the boy whom I attended at Meerut, many years ago, when you and your Sahib were living near the Begum's bridge?'

The poor woman looked at him for a moment, then repeated his name, and burst into tears. Her recollections crowded before her too thickly to admit of her dissembling any further with her visitor; and she admitted that she was the widow of Captain Gay, of her Majesty's —— Regiment of Foot.

The doctor was under no promise to Ellen to keep his discovery secret; and feeling at liberty to speak of it, did so publicly as well as in private. The peerages were looked into, and Black and Blue's pedigree examined. There were the names of all the late lord's sons, and sure enough there was Francis's name above that of Frederick's, the present earl; opposite to the name of Francis were the letters signifying, 'died unmarried.' Black and Blue of course became an object of great curiosity. His right to a title did not induce him to alter his prices in any way, and hence he was kicked and cuffed, and abused as much as ever, by the young lieutenants and ensigns, who, by-the-bye, always addressed him as 'my lord,' and 'your lordship.'

'Pomatum, my lord! Pomatum, did you say? Yes! But let me smell it. O! your lordship calls this pomatum! I call it hog's lard washed in sandalwood water. How much? One rupee! O, you villanous peer of the realm! are you not ashamed of yourself?'

Another would thus address him:

'Look here, Lord Black and Blue. Why don't you go home and upset your uncle? Turn him out of his title and estates—eh? You would be sure to marry some beautiful girl.'

To this Black and Blue would respond:

'What do I want with title and beautiful gal! This is my home, and I got good business, good many friends, and two or three very beautiful gal.'

'Where, Black and Blue?'

'Ah! that is my business.'

'Well, what will you sell your title for?'

'Well, what you offer?'

'One hundred rupees' (10*l.*)

'Say one hundred and twenty-five.'

'No.'

'Well, take it—there. Give money, and I give receipt. You write it out; I sign it. Sold one title to Ensign Matheson for a hundred rupees.'

'But there are two titles, you ass; one an earldom, and the other a viscounty.'

'Well, you take the two; give two hundred rupees for both.'

'No. The one I have already bought is the biggest and of the best quality; the other is the small one, and of inferior quality.'

'Well, I make reduction in price; take one with the other, and give me one hundred and seventy-five rupees. That can't hurt anybody that wants a title.'

Would any of these lads, who had nothing in the world beyond their pay, have consented to an union between Black and Blue and one of their sisters, after he had come into what were his rights? No! Would the poorest and most unprincipled officers—civil and military—in the whole of India? No! Would any European girl of respectability who had lived in India, to say nothing of the daughters of gentlemen and ladies, have wedded the black heir to the title and estates of the Earl of Millflower? No. Not in India could his sable lordship have found a virtuous white woman to accept his hand!

In due course the story of Black and Blue's birth crept into the columns of one of the Calcutta newspapers, and ere long an attorney of the Supreme Court paid a visit to the imperial city, and had an interview with Black and Blue. He proposed to the box-waller to take him to England, and establish his claim to the estates, which he truthfully represented as worth more than half a million sterling—fifty lacs of rupees. He, the attorney, would pay all expenses of the suit, and in the event of success, which was certain, would receive only five per cent. or fifty thousand pounds, leaving Black and Blue a balance of forty-five lacs.

Black and Blue, who loved and adored money, on hearing such a sum spoken of, rolled his blue eyes and red tongue, and almost fainted. But then, to cross the black water!—as the natives call the ocean—that thought made him shudder and shake his head.

The attorney represented to him that he should live in great comfort during the voyage; that the best cabin in the ship should be taken for him; that he should have servants about him; and drawing forth a number of prints of English beauties, he exhibited them to the gaze of Black and Blue.

Black and Blue said he would consult his European friends. He did so, and many of those friends dissuaded him from going to England. Not that they had any doubt as to the issue of his claim, if it should be disputed; but upon the reasonable ground that he was very happy where he was. Others advised him to go by all means, and take up his title and the wealth that pertained to it. His mother entreated him not to leave her. But in the end the voice of the attorney prevailed, and Black and Blue declared himself ready to accompany him.

Ten thousand rupees (one thousand pounds) were given to Ellen for her support during the temporary absence of her son, who was to return as soon as he had realized his forty-five lacs (four hundred and fifty thousand pounds). It was said that a mercantile firm in Calcutta, in which an illustrious native gentleman was a partner, advanced the means required for the purpose of establishing the black man's right to the earldom.

The attorney possessed himself of the proofs. He had the papers of the Honourable Francis Gay, amongst which were letters from the late Lord Millflower to his eldest brother, Lord Larkspeare. He also, in the presence of credible witnesses, received from the hands of Ellen the dead man's uniform; secondly, he had the deposition on oath of the superintending surgeon, and of several other officers who were cognizant of every particular. Many gave these depositions with reluctance, but felt bound to speak the truth when interrogated. In a word, the attorney got his case up remarkably well.

Black and Blue and the attorney left Calcutta in one of the large passenger ships, and in the month of April landed at Gravesend, whence they journeyed to London. Here Black and Blue was prevailed upon to wear Christian clothes. In his snow-white muslin dress, his pink turban, and his red slippers covered with gold embroidery, Black and Blue had looked an aristocratic native, notwithstanding he was so very black. [Colour is no criterion of high caste or rank in India. The late Maharajah Rooder Singh, of Darbungah, whose family—to borrow a phrase from 'Burke's Peerage'—is one of stupendous antiquity, had the complexion of an African; while his younger brother, Basdeo, who now sits on the throne, is far fairer than his Highness the Maharajah Dulleep Singh.] But in his black trousers, black waistcoat, black surtout coat, white neckcloth, black beaver hat, and Wellington boots, poor Black and Blue looked truly hideous; while his slouching Indian gait would have led most people to conclude that he was intoxicated.

Poor Black and Blue had never tasted anything stronger than water in the whole course of his life.

The attorney had an interview with Frederick Earl of Millflower. He wrote to the firm in Calcutta to that effect, and he further stated that the Earl had set him at defiance, and that he was about to institute a suit in the proper court.

This was the last that was ever heard in India of Black and Blue, or of the attorney. Inquiries were instituted, but with no avail. There were many conjectures; the one most generally entertained was, that poor Black and Blue and his undoubted claim were disposed of by the attorney for a sum which satisfied him, and that Black and Blue was secretly led into indulgences in some foreign country and died of their effects. But his mother, who is still living, will not believe that he is dead, and feels convinced that some day or other he will turn up and be restored to her.

'What on earth became of that black earl?' is a question very often put by many who were acquainted with his strange history.

The Mahommedan Mother

MUSSOORIE AND LANDOUR, situated in the lower range of the Himalaya mountains, form the favourite sanitarium of the upper part of India. The scenery is more beautiful than that of Simlah; for Mussoorie and Landour command a view of Dehra Dhoon, which resembles (except that the Dhoon is grander and more extensive) the plains of Italy as seen from the ascent of the Simplon. The mall of Mussoorie is crowded every evening with visitors; some on horseback, some on hill ponies, some on foot, and some in the janpan (something like a sedan-chair carried by four hill men). A gayer scene it would be impossible to conceive. Every one knows his neighbour; and, in passing along the narrow road, stoppages are frequent. Compliments must be exchanged, and the news or scandal of the day gossiped about. Every now and then you hear a cry of 'What a shame!' from a terrified lady in a janpan, while a couple of lovers gallop past on spirited Arabs at full speed. Sometimes a shriek from a nervous mamma reverberates through the valleys, when she beholds her children in the way of the heedless pair.

Accidents sometimes occur. A few years ago, a lady and a gentleman were riding round a place called the Camel's Back;

The Mahommedan Mother

the road gave way, and they fell down a precipice several hundred feet. The horses were killed, but the riders miraculously escaped with only a few severe bruises. On another occasion, a gentleman of the civil service was taking his evening walk, when one of his dogs ran between his legs, and precipitated him. He was killed on the spot.

On the mall every evening was to be seen a native woman standing by the side of the road, near a large rock, watching those who passed by. She was well dressed, and her face was concealed, according to the custom of persons of her apparent station in life. There she stood, attracting general attention. She was a woman of slight, but graceful figure, and rather tall. Many persons were curious to know who she was, and to see her face; but she took care that in this respect none should be gratified. Sometimes she would go away early; at other times she would remain until it was quite dark. Some suspected—and I was amongst the number—that she was the native wife of some European officer who had divorced himself, and visited the 'Hills,' whither the woman, to annoy, had followed him; and there was no small amount of speculation as to whose wife she could be. Some of the guesses, if they were seriously made, were extremely ungenerous, for they included several elderly officials, who could not by any possibility have been married to this mysterious lady. I was determined to know who she was; and one night, when most people were thronged around the band, I approached her, and inquired if I could be of any service to her. She replied (her face closely covered), 'Yes; by going away.' She had a very sweet voice, and its sorrowful tones inspired me with pity, when she added, 'I am a poor woman; my heart is crushed; do not add to my misery by remaining near me.' I obeyed her, after apologizing for having intruded. Several other persons had attempted to extract some particulars from the lady, and had received the same sort of reply as that she had given to me.

The rains were about to commence, and storms were not unfrequent. The mall was less frequented; only a few—those who cared little about hearing 'heaven's artillery thunder in the skies,' or being pelted by hailstones as large as marbles—ventured out; but amongst that few was the native lady, who, punctual as the light of day, visited that huge, dismal-looking rock, and gazed upon the road.

I have seen a storm on the heights of Jura—such a storm as Lord Byron describes. I have seen lightning and heard thunder in Australia; I have, off Terra del Fuego, the Cape of Good Hope, and the coast of Java, kept watch in thunderstorms which have drowned in their roaring the human voice, and made every one deaf and stupified; but these storms are not to be compared with a thunderstorm at Mussoorie or Landour.

In one of these storms of thunder, lightning, wind, and hail, at about five o'clock in the afternoon, I laid a wager with a friend that the native lady would be found as usual standing near the rock. Something secretly assured me that she was there at that moment, looking on unmoved, except by the passions which had prompted her pilgrimage. How were we to decide it? 'By going to the spot,' I suggested. My friend declined; but declared that, as far as the bet was concerned, he would be perfectly satisfied with my word, either one way or the other; namely, whether I had won or lost.

I set off upon my journey. The rock was at least three-quarters of a mile distant from my abode. My curiosity was so much aroused—albeit I felt certain the woman was there—that I walked through the storm without heeding it. Every now and then I saw the electric fluid descend into a valley; then heard that strange noise which huge pieces of rock make when they bound from one precipice to another, tearing up trees, and carrying large stones and the earth along with them in their headlong career; but still my mind was intent on the woman, and nothing else.

Was she there?

Yes; there she sat, drenched to the skin; but I could not pity her wet and cold condition, for I could see that she cared no more about it than I cared about my own. She drew her garment so closely over her face, that the outline of her features was plainly discernible. It was decidedly handsome; but still I longed to see her eyes, to confirm my impression. I sat beside her. The storm still raged, and presently the lady said, 'The heaven is speaking, Sahib.' I answered, 'Truly; but the lightning, the parent of that sound which I now hear, I cannot see.' She understood me, and gave me a glimpse of her eyes. They were not like the eyes of a native; they were of a bluish hue, almost grey. I said to her, in Hindoostanee, 'You are not a native; what do you do here in a native dress?'

'I would I were an European,' she answered me. 'My feelings, perhaps, would be less acute, and I should be sitting over a bright fire. Oh, how loudly the heaven is speaking! Go home, Sahib, you will catch cold!'

'Why do *you* not go home?' I asked. 'You will see no one to-day. No—not even your beloved. I am the only being who will venture out in a storm like this; and I do so only for your sake.'

'My heart is as hard as this rock,' she said, flipping her finger against the granite, 'to all except one being—a child. Oh, how the heaven is speaking, Sahib!'

'Do you not fear the lightning and the hail?' I asked her.

'I did once,' she replied. 'I trembled whenever it came near; but now, what does it signify? *Bidglee* (lightning), come to me,' she cried, beckoning to a streak of fluid which entered the ground within a hundred yards of us. '*Bidglee*, come here, and make a turquoise of my heart.'

What pretty feet! She had kicked off her shoes, which were saturated and spoiled.

'Go home, Sahib' (such was the refrain of her conversation); 'you will catch cold!'

By degrees I had an opportunity of seeing all her features. She was most beautiful, but had evidently passed the meridian of her charms. She could not have been less than twenty-four years of age. On the forefinger of her left hand she wore a ring of English manufacture, in which was set a red cornelian, whereon was engraved a crest—a stag's head.

I took her hand in mine, and said, 'Where did you get this?' pointing to the ring.

She smiled and sighed, and then answered, 'Jee (sir), it belonged to an Ameer (a great man).'

'Where is he?'

'Never mind.'

'Do you expect to see him soon?'

'No; never.'

'Is he old?'

'No; not older than yourself. How the heaven is speaking!'

'Let me see you to your home.'

'No. I will go alone.'

'When do you intend to go?'

'When you have left me.'

'You are very unkind thus to repulse my civility.'

'It may be so; but my heart's blood is curdled.'

I bade her farewell; and through the storm, which still raged, I went home and won my wager.

I could not rest that night. The beautiful face of the native woman haunted me. In vain I tried to sleep, and at last I arose from my bed, and joined a card-party, in the hope that the excitement of gambling would banish her from my brain. But to no purpose. I knew not what I was playing, and ere long I left off in disgust.

Almost every one who visits the Hills keeps a servant called a *tindal*. His duty is to look after the men who carry your janpan, to go errands, to keep up the fire, and to accompany you with a lantern when you go out after dark. These tindals, like the couriers on the Continent, are a peculiar race; and, generally speaking, are a very sharp, active, and courageous people. I summoned my tindal, and interrogated him about the native lady who had caused so much sensation in Mussoorie. The only information he could afford me was, that she had come from a village near Hurdwar; that she was rich, possessed of the most costly jewels, kept a number of servants, moved about in great state on the plains, and, for all he knew, she might be the wife or slave of some Rajah.

Could she, I wondered, be the famous Ranee Chunda, the mother of Dulleep Singh, and the wife of Runjeet?—the woman who, disguised as a soldier, had escaped from the fort of Chunar, where she had been imprisoned for disturbing, by her plots, the imagination of Sir Frederick Currie, when he was Resident at Lahore? The woman I had seen and spoken to 'answered to the description' of the Ranee in every respect, excepting the eyes. Dulleep Singh was living at Mussoorie, and he not unfrequently rode upon the mall. Ranee Chunda had a satirical tongue, and a peculiarly sweet-toned, but shrill voice, and she had remarkably beautiful feet, and so had this woman. Ranee Chunda had courage which was superhuman; so had this woman. Ranee Chunda had a child—an only child; so had this woman.

I asked the tindal where the lady lived. He replied, that she occupied a small house near the bazaar, not very far from my own abode. 'She is in great grief,' the tindal yawned, 'about something or other.'

'Endeavour to find out the cause of her misfortunes,' said I, 'and you shall be rewarded according to your success.'

Next day the tindal reported to me that I was not the only Sahib who was deeply interested in the native lady's affairs; that many wished to make her acquaintance, and had sent their tindals to talk to her; but that she had firmly and laconically dismissed them all, just as she had dismissed him—' Tell your master that the sufferings of an object of pity, such as I am, ought not to be aggravated by the insulting persecution of gay and light-hearted men.'

The day after the storm brought forth the loveliest afternoon that can be imagined. The sun shone out brightly, the clouds were lifted from the Dhoon, and the vast panorama resembled what we read of in some fairy tale. All Mussoorie and Landour turned out. The mall was so crowded, that it was difficult to thread one's way through the throng.

Was the lady at the rock? Yes; there she stood, as usual, watching those who passed. The Maharajah with his suite appeared. I was convinced that the woman was the Maharajah's mother; but I did not breathe my suspicions, lest I might cause her to be arrested. When it became dusk, and the visitors were taking their departure, I again approached the lady, and made my 'salaam,' in that respectful phrase which is always adopted when addressing a native woman of rank. She at once recognised me as the person who had spoken to her during the storm on the previous afternoon, for she alluded to its fury, and said she had taken a wrong road, had lost her way after I had left her, and did not reach home till nearly midnight. She concluded her little speech with a hope that I had been more fortunate.

'You should have allowed me to escort you,' said I. 'I would have helped to carry your load of sorrow.'

She looked at me, and suddenly and abruptly said, 'Your name is Longford.'

'You are right,' said I.

'About three or four years ago you stayed for several days with a friend in a tent near Deobund? You were on your way to these mountains?'

'I did.'

'You had a little dog with you, and you lost it at Deobund?'

'I did lose my dog, and made a great noise about it. But how do you know all this?'

She smiled and sighed.

I was bewildered. My belief that she was the Ranee Chunda was almost confirmed. It was close to the encampment of the Ranee, when she was on her way to Chunar, that my dog was lost, and my servants and the officers of police declared that it must have been some of the Ranee's people who had stolen the favourite.

'The dog is still alive,' said the lady; 'and if you will come to-morrow, at twelve o'clock, to my house, you shall see him; but you will promise not to take him from me?'

'Of course I will not take him from you. But let me see him to-night, and tell me how he came into your possession. I will see you to your home.'

'No, Sahib; be patient. I will tell you all to-morrow; and, when you have heard my story, you will perhaps do me a kindness. It is in your power to assist me. Tell me where you live, and I will send my brother to you at eleven o'clock. He will conduct you to my house. Salaam, Sahib.'

I returned her salaam, and left her.

I did not go to bed till two o'clock the next morning, and when my tindal aroused me at eleven, and informed me that a young man wished to see me, I was disposed to believe that my engagement at twelve had been made in my dreams.

I ordered the young man to be admitted. He came to my bedside, and said in a confidential tone of voice: 'The lady has sent me to wait your commands.' I got up, made a hasty toilet, drank a cup of very hot tea, and followed the young man, who led me to the little house near the theatre, at the top of the Bazaar. I entered the abode, and found the lady sitting, native fashion, on a carpet on which was strewed marigold and rose leaves. Her silver kulean (small hookah) was beside her; and, sure enough, there was my long-lost terrier, Duke, looking as sleek, fat, lazy, and useless as a native lady's dog could be. After expressing my thanks to the lady for her condescension in granting me the interview, I spoke to my former favourite, Duke, but he only stretched himself, and yawned in reply.

'And you have still that ring with the blue stone in it,' said the lady, taking my hand, and smiling while she looked at the ring. 'I remember observing this when I saw you asleep, one morning, on a couch in the tent at Deobund. Had I noticed it when you addressed me during the storm, I would not have spoken so rudely to you.'

'I do not remember having seen you previous to the other evening,' said I; 'and if I had, I should never have forgotten it. Where have we met?' I repeated.

'Where I had opportunities of seeing you, but where you could not see me.'

There was an old serving woman, whom she called mother, attending upon her, and the young man whom she called brother, a soldier-like looking youth, was still standing in the room to which he had conducted me. The lady desired them both to withdraw, and then begged me to bring the mora (or stool) upon which I was sitting close to her side. I obeyed her. She placed her finely-formed head in the palms of her hands, and gave vent to a violent flood of tears. I suffered her to weep without interruption. Grief appeared to relieve her rather than to increase her pain. At length she dried her eyes, and said:—

'My father was a *Moolvee* (Mahommedan law officer), attached to the Sudder Court, in Agra. I am his only daughter. He was absent from home all day. Why should he not be? He was paid for it; he ate the Company's salt. Well, when I was about fifteen years of age I was enticed away from my home by the *Kotwall* (native police officer). He sent an old woman, who had silver on her tongue and gold in her hand. She told me long stories about love; and promised me that if I left my home I should marry the *Kotwall's* son, who was young and handsome. I was but a child and very foolish. The servants who had charge of me were all bribed heavily. One received three hundred rupees, another two hundred, a third one hundred. These people encouraged me in the idea that to marry the *Kotwall's* son would be the most prudent thing in the world; and, one day, when my father had gone to the Court at about ten o'clock, I eloped with the old woman whom the *Kotwall* had sent to talk me over.

'We travelled all day in a *bylee* (native carriage), guarded by two sowars. I asked the old woman several times where she was taking me, but her only reply was, 'Set your heart at rest, child, and eat some sweetmeats.' The *pawn* which she gave me must have been drugged, for shortly after eating it I fell asleep. How long I slept I cannot say, but when I awoke I found myself in the house of a Sahib. The old woman was there also. I became alarmed, but my fears were quieted by the old woman's tongue. She told me I was close to Agra, but the truth was, I was one hundred koss (two hundred miles) distant. Nautch girls were sent for, and they danced before me. I had this hookah given to me, and these bangles. A boy very handsomely dressed waited upon me, and brought my food. Parrots, minahs, and doves were purchased for me to play with. Whatever my childish fancy dictated the old woman instantly procured.

'I was so constantly amused, I had no time or inclination to think of my home. My father was a bad-tempered man, and I was only too glad to be out of hearing of the quarrels in which he constantly engaged with his servants and dependents. One evening the old woman said to me, 'Baba (child), order a Nautch this evening, and let me, in your name, invite the Sahib to witness it.' I had never seen an Englishman—an European—except at a distance. The idea of being in the room with one inspired me with terror. I had been taught to despise the Kafir, whom my father said he was compelled to serve. I objected; but the old woman's eloquence again prevailed.

'The night came; I was seated on my *fureesh* (carpet) just as I am now, and dressed in clothes of the gayest description. I was like a little queen, and felt as proud as was Noor Jehan. I was then very handsome. If I had not been, much trouble would have been spared; and my flesh was firm—not as it is now. At about ten o'clock the Sahib made his appearance. When he came into the room I was ready to faint with alarm, and, turning my head away, I clung to the old woman, and trembled from head to foot. '*Dhuro mut*' (do not fear), said the Sahib; and then he reproved, but in a gentle voice, the Nautch girls who were laughing loudly at me. The old woman, too, bade me banish my fears. After a while, I ventured to steal a look at the Sahib; and again averted my face, and clung to the old woman. The Sahib, after remaining a brief while, during which he praised my beauty, retired, and I was once more happy. 'There,' said the old woman, when he was gone; 'you see the Sahib is not a wild beast out of the jungles, but as gentle as one of your own doves.'

'On the following day I heard the Sahib talking in the next room; I peeped through the keyhole of the door, and saw him seated at a table. The *nazir* (head clerk) was standing beside him, reading. There was a man in chains surrounded by *burkandâzes* (guards) at the other end of the room, and a woman was there giving her evidence. The Court-house was undergoing some repairs, and the Sahib was carrying on his magisterial duties in his dining-room. The man in chains began to speak, and deny his guilt. The Sahib called out, '*Choop!*' (Silence!) in a voice so loud, that I involuntarily started back and shuddered. The prisoner again addressed the Sahib, and one of the *burkandâzes* dealt him a severe blow on the head, accompanied by the words, '*Suer! Chor!*' (Pig! Thief!) The case was deferred until the following day, and the court closed at about four o'clock in the afternoon, when the Sahib again paid me a visit.

'I was now afraid to show my fears, lest the Sahib should order me to be killed; and I therefore put on a cheerful countenance, while my heart was quivering in my breast. The Sahib spoke to me very kindly, and I began to dread him less.

'In this way I spent a fortnight; and, at the end of that time, I ventured to talk to the Sahib as though I were his equal. It afforded me great amusement to watch the administration of justice through the keyhole; and, young as I was, I imbibed a desire to have a share in the arbitrary power which was daily exercised.

'One day, when the Sahib came into my room, I began to talk to him about a case of which he had just disposed. He laughed, and listened to my views with great patience. I told him that the evidence upon which the prisoner had been convicted was false from beginning to end. He promised me that he would reverse the sentence of imprisonment; and, in the ecstasy of my joy at finding that I really had some power, I was intoxicated and unconscious of what I was doing. I suffered the Sahib's lips to touch mine. No sooner had I done so than I felt a degraded outcast, and I cried more bitterly than I have words to describe. The Sahib consoled me, and said that his God and his Prophet should be mine; and that in this world and the next our destinies should be the same.

'From that day I was a wife unto him. I ruled his household, and I shared his pleasures and his sorrows. He was in debt; but, by reducing his expenses, I soon freed him, for his pay was fifteen hundred rupees a month. I suffered no one to rob him, and caused the old woman, who was a great thief and cheat, to be turned away. I loved him with all my soul. I would rather have begged with him than have shared the throne of Ackbar Shah. When he was tired, I lulled him to sleep; when he was ill, I nursed him; when he was angry, I soon restored him to good-humour; and, when I saw him about to be deceived by subordinates, I put him on his guard. That he loved me I never had any reason to doubt. He gave me his confidence, and I never abused his trust.'

'Who was the man?' I inquired; for I was in doubt, although I suspected.

'Be patient, Sahib,' she replied, and then resumed. 'At the end of two years I became a mother.'

Here she gave vent to another flood of tears.

'The Sahib was pleased. The child seemed to bind us more closely together. I loved the child; I believe it was because it bore such a strong likeness to its father. When the Sahib was away from me on duty in the district, he seemed still by my side, when I looked at the boy, who was as white as you are.'

'Is the child dead?' I asked.

'Be patient, Sahib. When you passed through Deobund, and stayed in the tent with your friend, my child was two years old. I was the mistress of that encampment at Deobund, and the wine you drank was given out with this hand.'

'How little do men know of each other!' I exclaimed; 'even those who are the most intimate! I had not the least idea there was a lady in the camp, I assure you.'

'How angry with you was I,' said she, 'for keeping the Sahib up so late. You talked together the whole night long. Therefore I had no remorse when I took your dog. Well, as you are aware, soon after that the Sahib was seized with fever, from which he recovered; but he was so shattered by the attack that he was compelled to visit Europe, where you know—' She paused.

A native woman will never, if she can avoid it, speak of the death of a person whom she has loved. I was aware of this, and bowed my head, touching my forehead with both hands. The father of her child had died on his passage to England.

'Before he left me,' she continued, 'he gave me all that he possessed; his house and furniture; his horses, carriage, plate; his shares in the bank; his watch, his dressing-case, his rings;—everything was given to me, and I own all to this hour. When I heard the sad news I was heartbroken. Had it not been for the child I would have starved myself to death; as it was, I took to opium and smoking *bhung* (hemp). While I was in this state, my Sahib's brother—the Captain Sahib—came, and took away the boy; not by violence. I gave it to him. What was the child to me then? I did not care. But the old woman whom you heard me call my mother, who now attends me, gradually weaned me from the desperation in which I was indulging; and, by degrees, my senses returned to me. I then began to ask about my child, and a longing to see him came over me. At first they told me he was dead; but when they found I was resolved to destroy myself by intemperance, they told me the truth; that the child was living, and at school in these hills. I have come hither to be near my child. I see him almost every day, but it is at a distance. Sometimes he passes close to where I stand, and I long to spring upon him and to hug him to my breast, whereon in infancy his head reposed. I pray that I could speak to him, give him a kiss, and bless him; but he is never alone. He is always playing with, or talking to, the other little boys at the same school. It seems hard that he should be so joyous while his own mother is so wretched. Of what use to me is the property I have, when I cannot touch or be recognised by my own flesh and blood. You know the master of the school?'

'Yes.'

'Could you not ask him to allow my child to visit you? I could then see him once more, and speak to him. You were a friend of his father, and the request would not seem strange.'

I felt myself placed in a very awkward position, and would make no promise; but I told the woman I would consider the matter, and let her know on the following day, provided she would stay at home, and not visit that rock upon the road any more. She strove hard to extract from me a pledge that I would yield to her request; but, difficult as it was to deny her anything—she was still so beautiful and so interesting—I would not commit myself, and held to what I had in the first instance stated.

~

I paid a visit to the school at which my friend's child had been placed by his uncle, a captain in the East India Company's service. I saw some thirty scholars, of all colours, on the playground; but I soon recognised the boy whom I was so curious to see. He was indeed very like his father, not only in face and figure, but in manner, gait, and bearing. I called to the little fellow, and he came and took my hand with a frankness which charmed me. The schoolmaster told me that the boy was very clever, and that, although only six years old, there were but few of his playmates whom he did not excel. 'His father was an old friend of mine,' I said. 'Indeed our acquaintance began when we were not older than this child. Would you have any objection to allow the boy to spend a day with me?'

'I promised his uncle,' was the schoolmaster's reply, 'that he should not go out, and that I would watch him closely; but of course he will be quite safe with you. Any day that you please to send for him he shall be ready.'

'Does he know anything of his mother?' I inquired.

'Nothing,' said the schoolmaster. 'He was very young when he came to me. I have no idea who, or what, or where the mother is, for his uncle did not enter into the particulars of his parentage. The mother must have been very fair, if she were a native, the boy is so very slightly touched with the tar-brush.'

I went home, and sent for the mother. She came; and I entreated her to forego her request, for the child's sake. I represented to her that it might unsettle him, and cause him to be discontented. I assured her that he was now as happy and as well taken care of as any mother could desire her offspring to be. On hearing this the poor woman became frantic. She knelt at my feet and supplicated me to listen to her entreaty—a sight of her child, a few words with him, and a kiss from his lips. She said she did not wish him to know that she was his mother; that if I would have him brought into my house, she would dress in the garb of a servant woman, or *syce's* (groom's) wife, and talk to the boy without his being aware that she was the person who had brought him into the world.

'And you will not play me false?' said I, moved by her

tears. 'You will not, when you have once got hold of the boy, decline to relinquish that hold, and defy his friends—as mothers *have* done—to take him from you, except by an order of Court? Remember, Dooneea (that was her name), that I am running a great risk; and am, moreover, deceiving the schoolmaster, and behaving badly to the boy's uncle, by allowing myself to be swayed by your tears and my own feelings. Consider what disgrace you will bring upon me, if you fail to keep your word in this matter.' She bound herself by an oath that she would do all I required, if I would only give her the longed-for interview.

'To-morrow, at twelve,' said I, 'you may come here. At that hour, in this room, the child shall be with me. Come in the dress of a poor woman, and bring an infant with you. Let your excuse be that you have come to complain of the ill-treatment you have received from your husband, who is in my service. This will give me an opportunity of bidding you remain until justice be done, and meanwhile you will see the boy; and when I go out of the room, which will be only for a short time, you can talk to him. Do you know your part, Dooneea?'

'Yes, Sahib.'

'To-morrow, at twelve. Salaam, Dooneea!'

'Salaam, Sahib.' She went away with a cheerful countenance.

There are no such actors in the world as the people of Hindostan. The boy came to me a little before twelve, and was reading to me, when Dooneea, with a child in her arms, and dressed in the shabbiest apparel, rushed into the room, and commenced an harangue. She said she had been beaten unmercifully by her husband, for no cause whatever; that he had broken one of her fingers, and had attempted to stab her; but she had saved her life by flight. All this she accompanied with gesticulations and tears, according to the custom of complainants in the East. I feigned to be very angry with the husband, and hastily left the room, as if to make inquiry and to send for him.

I ran round to an outer door, and peeped in upon Dooneea and her boy. She was repeating the same tale to the child, and the child was imploring her not to cry. It was a strange scene. The tears she was now shedding were not mock tears. The boy asked her how her husband came to beat her? She began thus:—' I was sitting near the fire talking to my eldest boy, and had my arm round his waist—there, just as I put my arm round your waist—and I said to the boy, 'It is getting very late and you must go to sleep,' and I pulled him to my breast—like this—and gave him a kiss on his forehead, then on his eyes—there—just as gently as that, yes, just like that. Well, the boy began to cry—'

'Why did he cry? Because you told him to go to bed?'

'Yes,' said Dooneea; 'but his father came in, and thought I was teasing the child. He abused me and then he beat me.'

The woman gazed at her child; and, having a good excuse for weeping in her alleged wrongs, she did not scruple to avail herself of it. From behind the screen which concealed me from her sight, and that of the boy, I, too, shed tears of pity.

I returned to the room, and said, 'Dooneea, since you are afraid of your life, do not leave this house until I tell you to do so; but give your infant to the sweeper's wife to take care of. I do not like your children in my house.'

How thankful she was! She placed her head upon my feet, and cracked her knuckles over my knees.

Charles Lamb says that the children of the poor are adults from infancy. The same may be said of the children of the rich in India. Dooneea's little boy discussed the conduct of the cruel husband, and sympathised with the ill-used wife, as though he had been called upon to adjudicate the affair in a court of justice. He even went so far as to say, 'What a wicked man to beat such a dear looking woman!' and he gave Dooneea the rupee which I had given to him on the day previous when I saw him at the school. With what delight did Dooneea tie up that piece of coin, from the child's hand, in the corner of her garment. It seemed far more precious to her than all the jewels which his dead father had presented to her in days gone by. It was a gift from her own child, who was living, but to her, dead. Dooneea spoke Persian—a language the boy did not understand. His father had taught Dooneea that language in order that their servants might not know the tenor of their discourse. In that language Dooneea now spoke to me, in the boy's presence.

'Is he not very like his father?' she said.

'Very,' I replied.

'Will he be as clever?'

'He is too young for any one to judge of that.'

'But he will be as generous' (she pointed to the coin), 'and he will be as tall, as good-looking, as passionate, as gentle, and as kind.'

The boy's boots were muddy. Dooneea observed this, and with her own little hands cleaned them; and smiling, she asked him for a present, in that tone and manner which the poorest menial in Hindostan adopts when addressing the most haughty superior.

The boy blushed, and looked at me.

'Have you nothing to give her?' said I.

'Nothing,' said he; 'I gave her my rupee.'

'Give her that pretty blue ribbon which is round your neck, and I will give you one like it,' said I.

He took the ribbon from his neck and gave it to Dooneea.

Dooneea twisted the ribbon in her hair, and began to weep afresh.

'Do not cry, you silly woman,' said I; 'I will see that your husband does not beat you again.'

She understood me, and dried her tears.

Dooneea again spoke to me in Persian. 'Sahib,' said she, 'they do not wash the children properly at that school. Order me to do this.'

'Charley, why did you come to me in this state, with your neck unwashed?' I asked the boy. 'We only wash in warm water once a week; on Saturdays,' he replied. 'This is Thursday.'

'But I cannot allow you to dine with me in this state,' said I, in Hindostanee. 'You must be well washed, my boy. Dooneea, give the child a bath.'

With reluctant steps, the child followed his mother to my bathing-room. I peeped through the purdah; for I began to fear that I should have some trouble in parting the mother from her child, and half repented that I had ever brought them together. While Dooneea was brushing the child's hair, she said, '*Toomara mama kahan hai?*—Where is your mother?'

The boy answered, 'I do not know.'

I began to cough, to inform Dooneea that I was within hearing, and that I objected to that strain of examination. She ceased immediately.

I had an engagement to ride with a lady on the Mall. My horse was brought to the door; but I was afraid to leave Dooneea alone with the boy, notwithstanding her solemn promise that she would not run off with him. Yet I did not like to hurry that eternal separation on earth which, for the boy's sake, I was determined their separation should be.

I walked up and down my verandah for some time, meditating how I could part them. At last it occurred to me that I would send the boy away to his school by stratagem, and trust to chance how I might best explain to Dooneea that he would not return. I ordered a *syce* (groom) to saddle a little pony that I possessed, and told Dooneea that I wished the boy to take a ride with me, and that while we were absent, she ought to take some food. It stung me to the soul to witness how innocent she was of my intentions; for she seemed pleased that I should show her child so much attention as to be seen in public with him.

As soon as we were out of sight of my house, I took the road for Landour, delivered the boy over to his schoolmaster, told my groom to keep the pony out till after dark, cantered to the Mall, kept my engagement, and returned to my home at about half-past seven o'clock. There was Dooneea waiting for us in the verandah.

'Where is the boy?' she inquired, on finding me return alone.

I gave her no reply; but dismounted and approached her. Taking hold of her wrists, I said, in the gentlest voice,

'Dooneea, I have fulfilled my promise. You have seen your child, you have spoken to him, you have kissed him. Enough. He has now gone back to school. You must not see him again, if you really love him.'

She trembled in my grasp, looked piteously in my face, gasped several times for breath, as though she longed to speak, and swooned at my feet. I lifted her, carried her into the house, and laid her upon my bed; then sent for servants, and for a doctor, who lived near my bungalow. The doctor came. While he felt her pulse, and placed his hand over her heart, I briefly explained to him what had taken place. He still kept his finger on the vein, and gazed on Dooneea's beautiful face. Blood began to trickle from her nostrils, and from her ears, staining the bed linen and the squalid garments in which she had attired herself. In a few minutes the doctor released his hold of her wrist. 'Poor thing!' he ejaculated. 'Her troubles are over! She is at rest!'

—— Never more on her
Shall sorrow light, or shame.

She was dead.

The old woman whom Dooneea called 'mother,' and the soldier-like looking youth whom she called 'brother,' decamped with her jewels and moveables, including my dog, 'Duke;' but the house near Hurdwar, and the bank shares—property to the value of about four thousand pounds—remain invested in the names of trustees for the benefit of the boy; who will, I trust, make good use of his little fortune, when he becomes of age.

Tirhoot, Lucknow, Bhitoor, etc

IT IS SOME years since I first landed in Calcutta. I was in no way connected with the Government, and was consequently an 'interloper' or 'adventurer.' These were the terms applied by certain officials to European merchants, indigo-planters, shopkeepers, artisans, barristers, attorneys, and others.

It was not long before I made up my mind to become a wanderer in the East. I had no occupation, was my own master, and had a large tract of country to roam about in. My first step was to acquire a knowledge of Hindostanee and of Persian. By dint of hard study, at the end of six months I found myself capable, not only of holding a conversation, but of arguing a point in either of these languages: and with a light heart I took my departure from the City of Palaces, and proceeded to Monghyr, on the Ganges.

The chief civilian of that district had invited me to spend a month with him. Every day I accompanied my friend to his court, and thereby got some insight into the administration of justice in India, both civil and criminal. Here, too, I first made acquaintance with Thugs. Several most notorious characters of that tribe were at Monghyr—not imprisoned, but permitted to move about. They had been pardoned on condition that they would become informers, and, to a certain extent, detectives, in the suppression of Thuggee in the British dominions. It was a curious feeling to be in conversation with men who had each committed his ninety or a hundred murders—to see the fingers that had strangled so many victims—to watch the process, for they were good-natured enough to act it. There was the unsuspecting traveller with his bundle; the decoy Thug, who engaged him in conversation; the two men, who, at the given signal, were to seize; the executioner, standing behind with the handkerchief, ready to strangle the victim. They even went through the operation of searching the 'deceased,' upon whom they found nothing in this case; but they assured me this frequently happened in reality. The reader is of course aware that it is a part of the Thug's religion not to rob a live body. The crime of murder must precede that of theft. The play—the tragedy—over (to these domesticated demons it was a mere farce), they laughed at the solemn expression which, I doubt not, was stamped upon my features.

These Thugs were permitted to have their families at Monghyr; and one morning when I strolled down to their camp, an old man made five children, the eldest boy not more than eight years old, go through the business of strangling and robbing a victim. In one respect these urchins outdid their progenitors in the acting. They not only went through the ceremony of searching the dead body, but, that done, they dragged it by the legs to a well, and, in dumb show, threw it down, and then uttered a prayer to Heaven.

'Was that good?' said one of the children, running up to

me for applause and a reward. I scarcely knew what to reply. Before I had time to give any answer, the child's father said, 'No; it was not good. You used the handkerchief before the signal was given. Go through it again, and remember, this time, that you must have patience.' The boys began again, much in the same spirit that an actor and actress would go through the strangling scene in 'Othello,' to please a fastidious manager.

Approaching a very interesting-looking woman, of about two-and-twenty years of age, I said to her, 'What do you think of this?'

She replied in a proverb: 'The mango always falls beneath the shade of the parent tree.'

'But the crime?' said I. 'What think you of that?'

She looked up with as lovely a pair of eyes as ever saw the light, smiled, and responded:

'Heaven will hold us all, Sahib!'

I was about to reason with her, but her husband, with an expression of pride, interfered, and informed me that she had taken eighteen lives.

'Twenty-one!' she exclaimed.

'Eighteen only!' said he.

'Twenty-one!' she persisted, and ran them over counting on her fingers the places and the dates when the murders were committed. Her husband then admitted that she was in the right, and, turning to me, remarked:

'She is a very clever woman, Sahib.'

'Were your victims men or women?' I said to her.

'All women,' she answered me. 'Some old and some young.'

I was tempted to ask her to show me how it was done; and after considerable coaxing she complied with my wishes. To my surprise she was the only actor in the scene, except the victim, with whom she went through the process of strangling with a piece of cord. The victim, another Thuggess, was supposed to be sleeping when the operation was performed, and I could not help admiring—horrible as the sight was— the accuracy with which she performed the throes and agony of death. To borrow an idea from Junius, 'None but those who had frequently witnessed such awful moments could describe them so well.'

At the house of my Monghyr friend I met a French gentleman, an indigo-planter of Tirhoot, in Behar. He invited me to pay him a visit, and to accompany him in his boat. He was about to sail on the following day. I say 'sail,' for at that time (the month of August), the country was inundated, and it would have been impossible to travel by land. I accepted the invitation, and we sailed from Monghyr to Hajeepore without going near the Ganges for several days.

Monsieur Bardon, the French planter, was one of the most accomplished and agreeable men I had ever met, and in truth one of the greatest characters. The hospitality of the Tirhoot planters is proverbial in India, and I believe I might have lived in that Garden of the East, as it is called, from that day to this, as a welcome guest of the various planters, if I had chosen still to be their guest. As it was, I was eight months in the district, and then had very great difficulty in getting away. A now celebrated officer, at that time commanding the Irregular Cavalry at Segowlie, induced me to visit him; and after leaving his abode, I went to the Bettiah Rajah, who initiated me into the mysteries of tiger-shooting. It was in the dominions of this small chief that my hands and face were so browned that I became far less fair than many natives of the country. Before leaving Tirhoot, however, I paid a visit to Rooder Singh, the Rajah of Durbungah, the richest native perhaps in all India. He has two hundred thousand pounds a year net revenue; and in a tank in his palace there is lying, in gold and silver, upwards of a million and a half sterling. Chutter Singh, the father of the Rajah of Durbungah, was a firm friend of the British Government during the Nepal war. He raised a regiment of horse and provisioned it. When asked by the authorities for his bill, he replied that the Government owed him nothing.

After leaving the Bettiah Rajah, I proceeded to Lucknow, where I improved myself greatly in Hindostanee. In this city, and in Delhi, the purest is spoken. At Lucknow I made the acquaintance of Ally Nucky Khan (the prime minister of the King of Oude, who is now imprisoned in Fort William), of Wuzy Ally Khan (a celebrity of Oude, who is since dead), and of Rugburdiall, the eldest son of the late Shah Beharee Lall, one of the richest bankers in India. Shah Beharee Lall is said to have died worth seven millions in cash; but I have reason to believe that three millions sterling was the utmost that he died possessed of. Rugburdiall held the office of treasurer to the King of Oude. Ally Nucky Khan gave me the idea of a man of small mental capacity, but of immense cunning and inordinate vanity. The late Mr. Beechy, the King of Oude's portrait-painter, must have taken at least a score of likenesses of Ally Nucky, who, to say the truth, is a remarkably good-looking personage. Wuzy Ally Khan was a tall and handsome man of about five-and-forty. His manners were refined, his address charming, and his bearing altogether that of a well-bred gentleman. Of his talents there could be no question; and he was, moreover, a learned and well-informed man. There could be no doubt that Wuzy Ally Khan, in point of fact, ruled the kingdom. The conversational powers of this man were immense, and he was both witty and humorous. A more agreeable companion it would be difficult to meet with in any country. When I first made his acquaintance, he was in great favour with the then resident at the court of Oude; but, on the appointment of Colonel Sleeman, he fell into disrepute with the British officials and continued so up to the time of his death, which occurred about two years ago. I was five months in Oude, and, during that period, spoke nothing but Hindostanee or Persian. I made a point of avoiding my own countrymen, and of associating only with the natives of India.

Previous to leaving Lucknow, a letter was despatched to Nena Sahib, informing him that a gentleman of distinction, a most intimate friend of the Governor-General, and related by birth or marriage to every member of the council in Calcutta, as well as a constant guest of the Queen of England, was travelling through Hindostan in disguise, and would most probably, by his presence, illumine the abode of Maharajah Bahadoor, and it was hoped that every respect would be paid to the dignity of the Sahib's exalted position, &c., &c. When the draft of this epistle was read aloud by the moonshee, who had written it from dictation, I expostulated, on the ground that the contents were not in accordance with the truth. My scruples, however, were eventually overcome, and I took leave of my Lucknow friends, after being provided with all that I should require on my journey (of about forty-five miles), and an escort of fifteen sowars (horsemen); for the road, at that time, between Lucknow and Cawnpore, was infested by robbers. About a mile from Bhitoor my palkee was placed upon the ground. I was asleep, but awoke, and inquired, 'Kia hua?' (What is the matter?)

I was informed by the bearers of my palkee that the Maharajah Peishwa Bahadoor had sent out an escort in honour of my approach, and presently there appeared at the door of my palkee a soldier-like looking Hindoo, who made me a very respectful salaam. The escort consisted of eight foot-soldiers with drawn swords, and four sowars. The former, running by the side of my palkee, encouraged the bearers to make haste; while the latter caused their horses to curvet and prance, and thus kick up a frightful dust. At the abode of the Maharajah Bahadoor, I was met by several of his musahibs (courtiers), who were exceedingly polite, and conducted me to a suite of apartments which had apparently been made ready for my reception; and so far as servants were concerned, I was literally surrounded. A sirdar bearer (personal attendant, or Indian valet) took charge of my two boxes which contained my wearing apparel. A khansamah (butler), followed by three khidmutghars (table servants), asked me if I would take some iced water, and in the same breath informed me that every kind of European drink was at hand. Brandy, gin, champagne, claret, sherry, port, beer, cherry-brandy and soda-water. And what would I take for dinner? Whatever the Sahib's heart might desire, was in readiness. Turkey? goose? duck? fowl? beefsteak? mutton-chop? ham and eggs? And here the khansamah (a venerable Mussulman) informed me, sotto voce, that the Maharajah was constantly in the habit of entertaining European gentlemen; and that, although his highness was himself a strict Hindoo, he had no kind of prejudice, so that if I preferred beef to any other kind of meat, I had only to give the order. I assured the khansamah that since my arrival in India, I had never tasted beef, or hog's flesh, and that if he would have prepared for me, as speedily as possible, some rice and vegetables, I should be quite satisfied. With a profound salaam the khansamah took his departure, followed by the khidmutghars. The sirdar bearers, and four other men, then approached me reverentially, and begged to conduct me to my sleeping apartment and the bathing-rooms.

There is something peculiarly quaint about the arrangement of European furniture in the house of a native gentleman. In the house of an European, the servants are, of course, taught how to arrange tables, chairs, and beds, according to European ideas; but it is otherwise with the servants of a rajah, or native gentleman. The consequence is that in the dining, or drawing-room, you will find a wash-hand stand, and a chest of drawers, and a toilet-table, while in the bedroom you will, perhaps, discover an old piano, an organ, a card-table, or cheffonier. The furniture has, for the most part, been purchased at various sales, and has belonged to officers of all grades, civil and military. There are the tent-table and the camp-stool of the dead ensign, in the same room with the marble-topped table and crimson damask covered easy chair of some luxurious judge. On the mantelpiece you will find a costly clock of the most elegant design and workmanship, and on each side of it, a pair of japan candlesticks, not worth half-a-crown. In this way are arranged the pictures on the walls. Immediately underneath a proof print of Landseer's 'Bolton Abbey,' or 'Hawking,' you will observe a sixpenny coloured print of the Duke of Wellington or Napoleon Bonaparte. The pictures, also, have been bought indiscriminately at various sales, and have been as indiscriminately suspended on the walls. There are the print-shop ballet girls intermingled with engravings of the most serious character. Fores's sporting collection with the most classical subjects. Foot-stools, musical-boxes, and elegantly bound books, writing-desks, work-boxes, plated dishes, sugar-basins, and teapots, are arranged in the most grotesque fashion imaginable. Upon an elegant mahogany sideboard you will find decanters and glasses of every description and quality. Upon another sideboard, in the drawing-room, you will find a variety of dinner-services, and earthen fragments thereof, all mixed.

There was but one set of rooms at Bhitoor for the reception of 'Sahib logue*,' and this was the set that I then occupied.

---

*The word 'logue' simply signifies people; but, when applied as above, it is nothing more than a plural. 'Sahib logue' (sahibs) 'mem logue' (ladies), 'baba logue' (children).

I had scarcely made myself comfortable, when the khansamah informed me that dinner was on the table. This was welcome intelligence, for I had not tasted food since morning, and it was half-past five p.m. I sat down to a table twenty feet long (it had originally been the mess table of a cavalry regiment), which was covered with a damask table-cloth of European manufacture, but instead of a dinner-napkin there was a bed-room towel. The soup—for he had everything ready—was served up in a trifle-dish which had formed part of a dessert service belonging to the 9th Lancers—at all events, the arms of that regiment were upon it; but the plate into which I ladled it with a broken tea-cup, was of the old willow pattern. The pilao which followed the soup, was served upon a huge plated dish, but the plate from which I ate it, was of the very commonest description. The knife was a bone-handled affair; the spoon and the fork were of silver, and of Calcutta make. The plated side-dishes, containing vegetables, were odd ones; one was round, the other oval. The pudding was brought in upon a soup-plate of blue and gold pattern, and the cheese was placed before me on a glass dish belonging to a dessert service. The cool claret I drank out of a richly cut champagne glass, and the beer out of an American tumbler, of the very worst quality.

I had not yet seen 'the Maharajah.' It was not until past eight that a moonshee came and inquired if I would have an interview with his highness. I replied that it would give me great joy, and was forthwith conducted through numerous narrow and gloomy passages to an apartment at the corner of the building. Here sat the Maharajah on a Turkey carpet, and reclining slightly on a huge bolster. In front of him were his hookah, a sword, and several nosegays. His highness rose, came forward, took my hand, led me to the carpet, and begged of me to be seated on a cane-bottomed arm-chair, which had evidently been placed ready for my especial ease and occupation. After the usual compliments had passed, the Maharajah inquired if I had eaten well. But, perhaps, the general reader would like to know what are 'the usual compliments.'

Native Rajah. 'The whole world is ringing with the praise of your illustrious name.'

Humble Sahib. 'Maharaj. You are very good.'

Native Rajah. 'From Calcutta to Cabul—throughout the whole of Hindoostan—every tongue declares that you have no equal. Is it true?'

Humble Sahib (who, if he knows anything of Asiatic manners and customs, knows that he must not contradict his host, but eat his compliments with a good appetite). 'Maharaj.'

Native Rajah. 'The acuteness of your perceptions, and the soundness of your understanding, have, by universal report, became as manifest as even the light of the sun itself.' Then, turning to his attendants of every degree, who, by this time, had formed a circle round me and the Rajah, he put the question, 'Is it true, or not?'

The attendants, one and all, declare that it was true; and inquire whether it could be possible for a great man like the Maharajah to say that which was false.

Native Rajah. 'The Sahib's father is living?'

Humble Sahib. 'No; he is dead, Maharaj.'

Native Rajah. 'He was a great man?'

Humble Sahib. 'Maharaj. You have honoured the memory of my father, and exalted it in my esteem, by expressing such an opinion.'

Native Rajah. 'And your mother? She lives?'

Humble Sahib. 'By the goodness of God, such is the case.'

Native Rajah. 'She is a very handsome woman?'

Humble Sahib. 'On that point, Maharaj, I cannot offer an opinion.'

Native Rajah. 'You need not do so. To look in your face is quite sufficient. I would give a crore of rupees (one million sterling) to see her only for one moment, and say how much I admired the intelligent countenance of her son. I am going to England next year. Will the Sahib favour me with her address?'

Humble Sahib. 'Maharaj.'

Here the Native Rajah calls to the moonshee to bring pen, ink, and paper. The moonshee comes, sits before me, pen in hand, looks inquiringly into my eyes, and I dictate as follows, laughing inwardly all the while: 'Lady Bombazine, Munnymunt, ka uper, Peccadilleemee, Bilgrave Isqueere, Sunjons wood-Cumberwill;' which signifies this: 'Lady Bombazine, on the top of the Monument, in Piccadilly, Belgrave Square, St. Johns Wood, Camberwell.' This mystification must be excused by the plea that the Rajah's assertions of his going to Europe are as truthful as Lady Bombazine's address.

The Maharajah then gives instructions that that document shall be preserved amongst his most important papers, and resumes the conversation.

Native Rajah. 'The Sahib has eaten well?'
Humble Sahib. 'Maharaj.'
Native Rajah. 'And drunk?'
Humble Sahib. 'Maharaj.'
Native Rajah. 'The Sahib will smoke hookah?'
Humble Sahib. 'The Maharajah is very good.'

A hookah is called for by the Rajah; and then at least a dozen voices repeat the order: 'Hookah lao, Sahib ke waste.' (Bring a hookah for the Sahib.) Presently the hookah is brought in. It is rather a grand affair, but old, and has evidently belonged to some European of extravagant habits. Of course, no native would smoke out of it (on the ground of caste), and it is evidently kept for the use of the Sahib logue.

While I am pulling away at the hookah, the musahibs, or favourites of the Rajah, flatter me, in very audible whispers. 'How well he smokes!' 'What a fine forehead he has!' 'And his eyes! how they sparkle!' 'No wonder he is so clever!' 'He will be Governor-General some day.' 'Khuda-kuren!' (God will have it so.)

Native Rajah. 'Sahib, when you become Governor-General, you will be a friend to the poor?'

Humble Sahib (speaking from the bottom of his heart). 'Most assuredly, Maharaj.'

Native Rajah. 'And you will listen to the petition of every man, rich and poor alike.'

Humble Sahib. 'It will be my duty so to do.'

Native Rajah (in a loud voice). 'Moonshee!'

Moonshee (who is close at hand). 'Maharaj, Protector of the Poor.'

Native Rajah. 'Bring the petition that I have laid before the Governor-General.'

The moonshee produces the petition, and at the instance of the Rajah, reads, or rather sings it aloud. The Rajah listens with pleasure to its recital of his own wrongs, and I affect to be astounded that so much injustice can possibly exist. During my rambles in India I have been the guest of some scores of rajahs, great and small, and I never knew one who had not a grievance. He had either been wronged by the government, or by some judge, whose decision had been against him. In the matter of the government, it was a sheer love of oppression that led to the evil of which he complained; in the matter of the judge, that functionary had been bribed by the other party.

It was with great difficulty that I kept my eyes open while the petition—a very long one—was read aloud. Shortly after it was finished, I craved permission to retire, and was conducted by a bearer to the sleeping-room, in the centre of which was a huge bedstead, a four-poster, but devoid of curtains. On either side were large looking-glasses in gilt frames, not suspended on the walls, but placed against them. Over the bed was a punkah, which was immediately set in motion. The movement of the punkah served a double purpose; it cooled the room, and drove away the mosquitoes. Having thrown myself on the bed, the bearer, who was in attendance, inquired if I would be shampooed. This was a luxury to which I was always partial, and, having signified that I desired it, four men were shouted for. Each took an arm or a leg, and began to press it, and crack the knuckle-joints of my fingers and toes. This continued until I had fallen asleep. I did not wake until eight o'clock on the following morning, when I was waited upon by the khansamah, who wished to know my pleasure with respect to breakfast. He informed me that he had 'Futnum and Meesum's,' Yorkshire pie, game pie, anchovy toast, mutton-chop, steak, sardines—in short, all that the Sahib logue were accustomed to take.

My breakfast over, and my hookah smoked, I lighted a cheroot, and walked out into a verandah, where I was soon joined by some of the Maharajah's favourites and dependents, who poured into my ear a repetition of the flattery to which I had listened on the previous night. It is not very tedious when you become used to it, and know that it is a matter of course, and is applied to every European guest of any real or supposed importance. Whilst thus engaged, smoking and listening, I was joined by the Maharajah, who held in his hand the *Delhi Gazette*, the *Mofussilite*, and the *Calcutta Englishman*. Of their entire contents he had been made acquainted by a half-caste, whom he kept (so he informed me) for the sole purpose of translating, orally, into Hindostanee, the Indian journals and the government gazettes, published in the English language. There was no occasion for me to read these papers, for the Maharajah gave me a very accurate resumé of them; having done this, he asked me to play a game of billiards. I am not a bad billiard-player; on the contrary, I have the vanity to think that I play remarkably well; but it was quite evident to me that the Maharajah did not play his best, and that he suffered me to beat him as easily as I did, simply out of what he considered to be politeness. All the while we were playing the favourites or courtiers of the Maharajah were praising us both. Neither of us made a stroke, good or bad, that did not bring down a shower of compliments. My impression is, that if I had run a cue, and cut the cloth at the same time, the bystanders would have shouted in praise of my skill and execution. I had already seen enough of native character to know exactly how I was to act. I feigned to be charmed with my success—childishly charmed. Whilst I was thus (to the delight of my host) ostensibly revelling in my triumph, the marker—a native, a Hindoo—took up a cue, and began to knock the balls about. He cannoned all over the table, went in off the red and white, screwed back under the cushion, and, in short, did whatever he pleased, and with perfect ease.

I could not help expressing to the Rajah my astonishment at the Hindoo marker's skill; whereupon, he informed me that, when he was a mere boy, he had been taught by the best player (an officer in the Light Cavalry) that ever came to India, and that for several years past he had been marker at various mess-rooms where billiards were played. The name of this Hindoo Jonathan was Runjeet. He was six-and-twenty years of age, about five feet five in height, remarkably slim, had a very handsome face, and eyes full of fire and spirit. He was for a long time marker to the Horse Artillery mess at Meerut, where I once saw him play a game with an officer celebrated for his skill. Runjeet gave his adversary sixty points out of a hundred, and won easily. What with his pay, or salary, the presents he received from gentlemen to whom he taught the game, and the gold mohurs that he occasionally had given to him when he won bets for his backers, Runjeet was in possession of some six hundred pounds a-year; but he was so extravagant in his habits, that he spent every anna, and died, I was told, 'not worth money enough to buy the wood to burn him.'

The Maharajah, on leaving the billiard-room, invited me to accompany him to Cawnpore. I acquiesced, and the carriage was ordered. The carriage was English-built—a very handsome landau—and the horses were English horses; but the harness! It was country-made, of the very commonest kind, and worn out, for one of the traces was a piece of rope. The coachman was filthy in his dress, and the whip that he carried in his hand was an old broken buggy-whip, which some European gentleman must have thrown away. On the box, on either side of the coachman, sat a warlike retainer, armed with a sword and a dagger. In the rumble were two other retainers, armed in the same manner. Besides the Rajah and myself there were three others (natives and relatives of the Rajah) in the vehicle. On the road the Rajah talked incessantly, and amongst other things that he told me was this, in reference to the praises that I bestowed on his equipage.

'Not long ago I had a carriage and horses very superior to these. They cost me twenty-five thousand rupees; but I had to burn the carriage and kill the horses.'

'Why so?'

'The child of a certain Sahib in Cawnpore was very sick, and the Sahib and the mem-Sahib were bringing the child to Bhitoor for a change of air. I sent my big carriage for them. On the road the child died; and, of course, as a dead body had been in the carriage, and as the horses had drawn that dead body in that carriage, I could never use them again.' The reader must understand that a native of any rank considers it a disgrace to sell property.

'But could you not have given the horses to some friend— a Christian or a Mussulman?'

'No; had I done so, it might have come to the knowledge of the Sahib, and his feelings would have been hurt at having occasioned me such a loss.'

Such was the Maharajah, commonly known as Nena Sahib. He appeared to me not a man of ability, nor a fool. He was selfish; but what native is not? He seemed to be far from a bigot in matters of religion; and, although he was compelled to be so very particular about the destruction of his carriage and horses, I am quite satisfied that he drank brandy, and that he smoked hemp in the chillum of his hookah.

It was half-past five o'clock when we arrived at Cawnpore. The officers, civil and military, and their wives, were just coming out for their evening drive on the mall. Some were in carriages, some in buggies, some on horseback. Every soul saluted the Maharajah; who returned the salute according to Eastern fashion—raising the hands to the forehead. Several gentlemen approached the carriage when it was drawn up near the band-stand, and inquired after the Maharajah's health. He replied that it was good and then introduced me to them in the following manner, and in strict accordance with the letter he had received from Lucknow: 'This Sahib who sits near me is a great friend of the Governor-General, and is a relation of all the members of Council—a constant guest of the Queen of England' (then came this addition of his own) 'and of both Houses of Parliament.' I need scarcely say that I wished my Lucknow friends had not covered me with such recommendations; for, wherever we went, and to whomsoever we spoke—no matter whether it was an European shopkeeper or an official magnate of Cawnpore— I was doomed to hear, 'This Sahib who sits (or stands) near me is a great friend,' &c., &c. Having exhibited me sufficiently in Cawnpore, the heads of the horses were turned towards Bhitoor, and we were dragged along the road at a slow pace, for the animals were extremely fatigued. The natives of India have no mercy on their cattle, especially their horses. During the ride back, I was again bored with the Rajah's grievance; and, to quiet him—for he became very much excited—I was induced to promise that I would talk to the Governor-General and the Council on the subject; and that if I did not succeed in that quarter, I would, on my return to England, take the earliest opportunity 'some day, quietly, after dinner' (this was his suggestion), of representing to her Majesty the exact state of the case, and that an adopted son of a Hindoo was entitled to all the rights and privileges of an heir born of the body. I furthermore promised him most solemnly that I would not speak to the Board of Control, or to the Privy Council on the subject; for the Maharajah assured me that he had the most positive proof that both these institutions had eaten bribes from the hand of the East India Company in respect of his claim. On probing him, however, I discovered that this positive proof was a letter from a villanous agent in England, who had written to him to say that 'the Company had bribed the Board of Control and the Privy Council, and that if his Highness expected to succeed, he must bribe over the head of the Company. Three lacs (thirty thousand pounds) would do it all.'

The Maharajah gave a nautch (native dance by women) that night.

On the following morning I awoke with a very bad headache, and in a philosophic mood. The various perfumes which had been sprinkled over my dress had somewhat overpowered me, and it may have been that the story told me in whispers by one of the three slaves who came to sing me to sleep had disordered my imagination. I was told that two women of rank were kept in a den not far from my apartments, and treated like wild beasts; and a third—a beautiful young creature—had recently been 'bricked up in a wall,' for no other fault than attempting to escape.

After breakfast, the Rajah showed me his elephants, his camels, his horses, his dogs, his pigeons, his falcons, his wild asses, his apes, his aviary full of birds, and all the rest of his curiosities. Then he exhibited his guns and pistols—by Purdey, Egg, and other celebrated makers—his swords, and his daggers, of every country and age, and when he had observed that he was very happy, under the influence of some stimulant recently imbibed, I took an opportunity of discoursing on the vanity of human wishes, and especially with reference to his Highness's grievance. I translated many sentiments of Juvenal and Horace into Hindoostanee; but, I regret to say, they had no effect on Nena Sahib.

The Upper Provinces

IT IS IMPOSSIBLE for an English gentleman to take his departure from the house of a native of India without giving a number of testimonials, in the shape of 'letters of recommendation' addressed to no one in particular. Nena Sahib had a book containing the autographs of at least a hundred and fifty gentlemen and ladies, who had testified in writing to the attention and kindness they had received at the hands of the Maharajah during their stay at Bhitoor. Having expressed my satisfaction as emphatically as possible in this book, the khansamah (house steward) demanded a certificate, which I gave him. Then came the bearer, the men who guarded my door, the coachman, the grooms, the sweeper. For each and all of these I had to write characters, and recommend them to such of my friends as they might encounter by accident or otherwise. It is a fearful infliction, this character writing; but every one is compelled to go through it.

I was now on my road to Agra, to pay a visit to a schoolfellow, who was then in the civil service, and filling an appointment in the station. It was in the month of September that I made the journey—the most unhealthy season of the year. Opposite to the first dâk bungalow, some twelve miles from the station of Cawnpore, I was stopped by a set of twelve palkee bearers, who informed me that a Sahib whom they were taking to Allyghur had been seized with cholera, and was dying in the bungalow. I hastened to the room and there found, stretched upon the couch, a young officer of about nineteen years of age.

His face was ashy pale, and a profuse cold perspiration stood upon his forehead. His hands and feet were like ice, and he was in very great pain. The only person near him was the sweeper, who kept on assuring me that the youth would die. As for the youth himself he was past speech, and I was disposed to think with the sweeper, that he was beyond cure. I administered, however, nearly a teaspoonful of laudanum in a wine-glass half-full of raw brandy, and then took a seat near the patient, in order to witness the effect. Ere long the severe pain was allayed, and the youth fell into a profound sleep, from which, I began to fear, he would never awake. To have administered a smaller dose at that stage of the disease would have been useless, for the body was on the very verge of collapse. Nevertheless, I began to feel the awkwardness of the responsibility which I had taken upon myself. Presently a palanquin carriage, propelled by bearers, came to the bungalow. An elderly lady and gentleman alighted, and were shown into a little room which happened to be vacant [A dâk bungalow has only two little rooms.] To my great joy I discovered that the new arrival was a doctor of a regiment, who, with his wife, was journeying to Calcutta. I was not long in 'calling in' the doctor; and I had the satisfaction of hearing him pronounce an opinion that the young ensign was 'all right,' and that the dose I had administered had been the means of saving his life. How readily, to be sure, do people in India accommodate each other. Although the doctor and his wife were hurrying down the country, and albeit the youth was pronounced out of danger, they remained with me until the following afternoon; when, having dined, we all took our departure together—the youth and I travelling northward, the doctor and his wife in the opposite direction.

The night was pitchy dark; but the glare from the torches rendered every object near to us distinctly visible. The light, shining on the black faces of the palkee bearers, they appeared like so many demons—but very merry demons; for they chatted and laughed incessantly, until I commanded them to be silent, in order that, while we moved along the road, I might listen to the ensign's story, which he told me in the most artless manner imaginable.

'I have only been six weeks in India,' he began, 'and at present only know a few words of the language. How I came into the Bengal army was this. My father was in the civil service of the Company, in the Madras Presidency; and, after twenty-one years' service, retired on his pension of one thousand pounds a year, and his savings, which amounted to twenty thousand pounds, and which were invested in five per cent government securities, so that his income was two thousand a year. We lived during the winter near Grosvenor-square: a house of which my father bought the lease for twenty years, and the summer we used to spend at a little place in Berkshire which he had bought. It was only a good sized cottage, and the land about it did not exceed three acres. But it was a perfect gem of a residence, and quite large enough for our family, which consisted of my father and mother, myself, and a sister who is a year and a half older than I am. I was at Harrow. My father intended that I should go to Oxford, and eventually be called to the bar. My sister had a governess, a very clever and accomplished girl, and the most amiable creature that ever lived. We were not an extravagant family, and saw very little company; but we had every comfort that a reasonable heart could desire, and I fancy that we lived up to the two thousand pounds a year. You see the education of myself and my sister was a heavy item. The governess had a hundred pounds a year, and then there was a singing master and a drawing master. About two years ago my father died, and my mother became almost imbecile from the excess of her grief. She lost her memory; and, for days together, knew not what she was doing.

Under my father's will she was entitled to all that he died possessed of, and was appointed his sole executrix. The house in South-street was given up, the unexpired portion of the lease disposed of, and the little place in Berkshire became our only home. My father's pension of course expired when he died, and we, the family, had now to live on the interest of the government securities. My mother, who was as ignorant as a child on all matters of business, was recommended to sell her government securities, and invest the proceeds in a joint-stock bank which was paying, and for more than a year did pay, eight per cent. But, alas, one wretched day the bank failed, and we were reduced suddenly from comparative affluence to poverty. The cottage, furniture, and all that my mother possessed, was seized, and sold. This happened only two years ago. Fortunately for me, my school education was pretty well completed; but of course the idea of my going to Oxford, and subsequently to the bar, was at once abandoned. My sister was obliged to take a situation as governess, in the family of a director of the East India Company: and through that gentleman's influence I obtained an ensigncy in the Native Infantry. The loss of her fortune, the parting with my sister (who is now on the Continent with the director's family) and myself, had such an effect upon my mother, that it was deemed necessary to place her in an asylum; where at all events she will be taken care of and treated with kindness. But I have my plans!' exclaimed the young man, who had just escaped the jaws of death. 'In ten years I will save enough to take me home to them; for, if I study hard—and I will do so—I may get a staff appointment, and——'

Here the bearers of my palkee informed me that two other travellers were coming down the road. They saw the light in the distance, more than a mile off, and they—the bearers—began to talk loudly and argue, that it was impossible for me to hear what the ensign was saying, and all attempts to silence them were vain. They were discussing, as they carried us along, whether they would exchange burdens with the down-coming bearers, insomuch as they were nearly midway between the stages. This is very often done by arrangement between them, and thus, in such cases, they get back more speedily to their homes. It was decided that the exchange should take place, if the other party were agreeable; for, on the down-coming travellers nearing us, the bearers of us—the up-going travellers—called a halt. Forthwith the four palkees were gently lowered till they rested on the ground. And now the chattering of the bearers became something awful. A native of Hindostan can settle nothing without a noise; and, as each palkee had twelve men attached to it besides the torch-bearers and those who carried our boxes, the number of voices, whooping, shouting, asserting, contradicting, scolding, and soothing, exceeded sixty. I and my companion, the ensign, shout to them to 'go on!' At length I got out of my palkee in a rage, and not only screamed at, but shook several of the black disputants. Whilst thus engaged, the doors of one of the downward palkees were opened, and a voice—that of a lady—thus greeted me, very good humouredly.

'My good sir, depend upon it that you are retarding your own progress, and ours, by attempting, so violently, to accelerate it. Pray let them settle their little affair amongst themselves.'

'I believe you are quite right,' I replied.

'Have you any idea of the hour?' she asked.

'Yes. It is about a quarter to twelve,' said I.

'I have lost the key of my watch; perhaps the key of yours would fit it.'

I hastened to my palkee, brought forth from beneath the pillow my watch and chain; and, taking them to the door of the lady's palkee, presented them through the opening.

'Thanks,' said the lady, after winding up her watch, 'thanks. It does very well,' and she returned the watch and chain. I saw, by the light of the torch, not only her hand—which was very small and pretty—but her face, which was more bewitching still, being lovely and young.

'Is there anything else you require?' I asked.

'Nothing. Unless you happen to have with you some fresh bread. My children, who are asleep in the other palkee, are tired of biscuits, and I imagine we shall not reach Cawnpore before mid-day to-morrow.'

It happened that I had a loaf in my palkee, and, with all the pleasure of which the heart of man is capable, placed it in the hands of the fair traveller. On this occasion she opened the doors of her palkee sufficiently wide to admit of my having a really good gaze at her beautiful features. She was enveloped in a white dressing-gown, and wore a hood made of black silk, and lined with pink. Her hair was brushed back off the forehead; but the long dark tresses came from behind the ears, and rested on her covered shoulders.

'Are you going to Agra?' she inquired.

'Yes,' I replied.

'Perhaps you would be good enough to return two books for me to the wife of the assistant magistrate. They will, no doubt, afford you as much amusement on your journey as they have afforded me. I finished them this afternoon, and they are now an encumbrance.' With these words she handed me the volumes, which I faithfully promised to return. By this time the bearers had settled their affair, and were ready to lift the palkees. I bade the fair traveller 'good night, and a safe journey.' We shook hands.

The reader may ask, 'Who was your friend?' I did not

know at the time. It was not until I had arrived at Agra that I was informed on this head. The books which she entrusted to my care I had not read; and, after parting with the ensign at the dâk bungalow at Bewah, they were, indeed, most agreeable companions. I have mentioned this little episode in my journey, not because there is anything in it worth recording, or because there is anything romantic therewith connected; but simply to show how readily we (Christians) in India obliged one another, albeit utter strangers, and how gladly we assist each other, whenever and wherever we meet. Such an episode in the journey of a traveller in India is one of its most commonplace incidents.

Since the news of the recent deplorable disasters has reached this country, many persons have expressed their surprise that a lady should be suffered to travel alone with her children, or be accompanied by no more than one female servant. The fact is, or rather was, that, on any dangerous road, a lady utterly unprotected was safer than a gentleman. The sex was actually its own protection. During my stay in India, I knew of at least a score of instances in which officers and civilians were stopped upon the roads, plundered, assaulted, and in one or two cases murdered, in the Upper Provinces; but I can only bring to mind two instances of European ladies having been molested. This is not to be attributed to any ideas of gallantry or chivalry on the part of marauders in the East; but simply to the fact that they knew the perpetrators of an offence committed against a lady would be hunted down to the death, while the sympathies entertained for the sufferings of a Sahib would be only those of an ordinary character, and soon 'blow over.' Even the palkee-bearers knew the amount of responsibility that attached to them, when they bore away, from station to station, a female burden; and, had the lady traveller been annoyed or interrupted by an European traveller, they would have attacked and beaten him, even to the breaking of his bones and the danger of his life, had he not desisted when commanded by the lady to do so. This has happened more than once in the Upper Provinces of India.

In December, eighteen hundred and forty-nine, the road between Saharumpore and Umballah was infested by a gang of thieves. Several officers had been stopped, robbed, and plundered of their money and valuables. I had been invited to Lahore, to witness the installation of Sir Walter Gilbert and Sir Henry Elliot as Knights Commanders of the Bath. The danger, near a place called Juggadree, was pointed out to me by a mail contractor, who, finding me determined to proceed, recommended me to dress as a lady for a couple of stages. I did so. I borrowed a gown, a shawl, and a nightcap; and, when I came near the dangerous locality, I put them on, and commanded the bearers to say I was a 'mem-Sahib,' in the event of the palkee being stopped. Sure enough, the palkee was stopped, near Juggadree, by a gang of ten or twelve armed men, one of whom opened the door to satisfy himself of the truth of the statement made by the bearers. The moment the ruffian saw my nightcap—a very prettily-frilled one it was, lent to me by a very pretty woman—likewise a small bolster, which, beneath my shawl, represented a sleeping baby, he closed the door, and requested the bearers to take up the palkee, and proceed; ay, and what was more, he enjoined them to be 'careful of the mem-Sahib!'

I have incidentally spoken of the installation of Sir Walter Gilbert and Sir Henry Elliot, in December, eighteen hundred and forty-nine. Eight years have not yet elapsed, and how many of the principal characters in that magnificent spectacle have departed hence! Sir Walter is dead; Sir Henry is dead. Sir Charles Napier and Sir Dudley Hill, who led them up to Lord Dalhousie, are dead. Colonel Mountain, who carried the cushion on which was placed the insignia of the order is dead. And Sir Henry Lawrence is dead; and poor Stuart Beatson. Alas! how many of that gay throng, men and women, husbands, fathers, wives, and daughters, who had assembled to witness the ceremony, have perished during the recent revolt in the Upper Provinces of India! Those who were present on that sixth of December eighteen hundred and forty-nine, and who, in eighteen hundred and fifty-seven, quietly reflect on what has occurred since, will scarcely believe in their own existence. It must appear to them—as it often appears to me—as a dream; a dream in which we saw Sir Charles Napier, with his spare form, his eagle eyes, his aquiline nose, and long grey beard, joking Sir Dudley Hill on his corpulence and baldness, and asking him what sort of figure he would cut now, in leading a forlorn hope? and Sir Dudley, proudly and loudly replying, that he felt a better man than ever. Presently, a meek civilian, in a white neckcloth, and ignorant of Sir Dudley's early deeds, was so unfortunate as to put the question:—

'*Did* you ever lead a forlorn hope, Sir Dudley?' a query

which induced Sir Dudley Hill to groan, previously to exclaiming—

'Such is fame! A forlorn hope, my dear sir! I have led fifty!'

This was, of course, an exaggeration; but I believe that Sir Dudley Hill had, in the Peninsular War, led more forlorn hopes than any other officer in the British army.

I have wandered away from the high road to Agra, and must return to it. I parted with the ensign at Bewah, and commenced reading the books which the then unknown lady had entrusted to my care. The day, towards noon, became hot, damp, and extremely oppressive; and there was no dâk bungalow, or other abode, within nine miles of me. Before long, I heard thunder in the distance, and presently the bearers communicated to me that a heavy storm was approaching, and that, in order to escape its fury, they wished to halt at a village just a-head of us. I consented, and was now hurried along the road at the rate of five miles an hour. My palkee was placed beneath a shed, and the bearers congregated around it. One of the number lighted his pipe (hubble-bubble), and passed it to his neighbour; who, after three whiffs, passed it to the next; who, after three whiffs, sent it on, until each had partaken of the smoke.

The little village, which was a short distance from the road, contained about sixty or seventy inhabitants, and about double that number of children of various ages. My presence excited no small degree of curiosity, and the whole of the villagers approached the shed, to have a look at me. The men and women, of course, were not alarmed, and looked on simply with that stupidity which is characteristic of the cultivators of the soil in the Upper Provinces of India. But it was otherwise with the more youthful, the children. They held aloof, and peeped from behind their parents, as if I had been some dangerous wild animal. My bearers wished to drive them all away; but I forbade this, partly because I had no desire to deprive the villagers of whatever pleasure a long inspection of me might afford them, and partly because I wished to sketch the group and listen to their remarks, which were chiefly of a personal character, and for the most part complimentary, or intended so to be.

A vivid flash of lightning, and an awfully loud clap of thunder, accompanied by a few large drops of rain, speedily dispersed the crowd, and I was left to myself and my bearers, who now huddled themselves together for warmth's sake. The air had become chilly, and even I was compelled to wrap my cloak and my blanket about my thinly-clad limbs. Another vivid flash of lightning, and another awful clap of thunder; then down came such hailstones as I had never seen before, and have never seen since in the plains of Hindostan. In size and weight they equalled those which sometimes fall in the Himalaya mountains in June and July. With these storms the rains usually 'break up,' and then the cold weather sets in, and with this season of the year, what climate in the world is superior to that of the Upper Provinces of India? When the thunder, lightning, and hail had ceased, and their continuance did not exceed fifteen minutes, the sun came out, and the face of heaven was as fair as possible, but the earth gave evidence of the severity of the storm. Not only was the ground covered with leaves and small branches, intermingled with the hail, but cattle and goats had been killed by the furious pelting of the huge stones; whilst the electric fluid had descended on one of the mud huts of the village in which I had taken refuge, and had stretched out in death an old man and two of his grandchildren, a boy of six years of age, and a girl of four. The parents of these children were absent from the village, and were not expected to return until the evening. On being informed of the accident, I expressed a desire to see the bodies, and was conducted by several of the villagers to the hut in which they were lying. I recognised at once the features of the old man who was a prominent figure in my sketch, and of one of the children, the little girl who held the old man so tightly by the hand while she peeped at me. The face of the boy had not struck me. There they were lying dead, but still warm, and their limbs, as yet, devoid of rigidity. The matter-of-fact way in which the natives of India regard the death of their relations or friends is something wonderful to behold. It is not that their affections are less strong than ours, or their feelings less acute. It is that fatality is the beginning and end of their creed. They are taught from their childhood to regard visitations of this character as direct and special acts of God— as matters which it is not only futile, but improper to bewail. None of the villagers—men, women, or children, exhibited any token of grief while gazing on the lifeless bodies they surrounded. And, on asking my bearers whether the parents of the children would weep when they returned, and found their offspring thus suddenly cut off, they replied, rather abruptly, 'Why should they weep at God's will?'

As I was preparing to leave the village, a middle-aged woman came up to me, and said:—

'Sahib, the parents of the dead children are very poor, and the expense of burning their remains will press very hard upon them. The wood for the old man will cost eight annas, and the fuel for each of the children four annas; in all, one rupee.'

I placed the coin in the woman's hand, and left, besides, a donation for the bereaved parents who were absent; having previously called several of the villagers to witness the proceeding. This I did at the suggestion of the palkee bearers, who entertained some doubts of the woman's honesty. We had not proceeded far, when I descried a small encampment beneath a clump of mango trees. It consisted of an officer's tent, and two long tents for native soldiers—Sepoys. One of these long tents was for the Hindoos, the other for the Mussulmans. When we came opposite to the encampment, I desired the bearers to stop, and to put some questions to a Sepoy who was standing near the road. I gleaned from him that the encampment was that of 'a treasure party,' consisting of a Lieutenant, and a company of native infantry, proceeding from Mynpoorie to Agra.

'Won't you go and see the Sahib?' asked the Sepoy.

'I don't know him,' said I.

'That does not signify,' said the Sepoy. 'Our Sahib is glad to see everybody. He is the most light-hearted man in Hindostan. His lips are the home of laughter, and his presence awakens happiness in the breast of the most sorrowful. His body is small, but his mind is great; and, in his eyes, the Hindoo, the Mussulman, and the Christian, are all equal.'

This description, I confess, aroused my curiosity to see so philosophical a Lieutenant, and it was not long before my curiosity was gratified; for he made his appearance at the door of his tent; and, observing my palkee, bore down upon it.

The Lieutenant wore a pair of white pyjamahs, which were tucked up to his knees, no shoes or stockings; a blue shirt, no coat, no jacket; a black necktie, and a leather helmet with a white covering, such as one sees labelled in the shop-windows 'for India.' His person was very small certainly, and the calves of his legs not bigger than those of a boy of twelve years of age. In his mouth he had a huge (number one) cheroot, and in his hand, a walking-stick, with a waist nearly as big as his own. Resting his chest upon this walking-stick, and looking me full in the face, perfectly ignorant, and seemingly indifferent, as to whether I might be a secretary to the government, or a shopkeeper, he thus familiarly accosted me:—

'Well, old boy, how do you feel after the shower?'

'Very well, I thank you.'

'Come in and have a cup of tea, and a round of toast, if you are not in a hurry to get on. It will set you up, and make you feel comfortable for the night.' This offer was so tempting, and so cordially made, that I was induced to accept it.

'Bring the Sahib into my tent, in the palkee,' said Lieutenant Sixtie to my bearers; and then addressing me, he remarked—'Don't get out. You'll wet your slippers.'

The bearers followed the Lieutenant, and put down my palkee upon two tiers of small boxes, which were spread over the space of ground covered by the tent.

'I was obliged to resort to this box dodge,' said my host, 'or I should have been drowned. I wish I owned only a quarter of this rhino we are treading on. If I did, catch me at this work any longer, my masters!' It was the treasure that the boxes contained, in all about twenty-five thousand pounds. 'Look here, old boy. Forego, like a good fellow, the tea and the toast. My servants will have such a bother to get a fire and boil water. Have some biscuits and cold brandy-and-water instead. You should never drink tea while travelling. It keeps you awake; and, what is more, it spoils the flavour of your cheroots. By the bye, have one of these weeds.'

I thanked my host; and, without any sort of pressing, yielded to his every wish—even unto playing *écarté* with him, while smoking his cheroots and drinking his brandy-and-water. The stakes were not very high. Only a rupee a game. During the deals, my host would frequently exclaim:

'By Jove! what a godsend it is to have some one to talk to for a few hours! I have been out for five days; and, during that time, have not uttered a word in my own language. Haven't had the luck to come across a soul. This escorting treasure is the most awful part of an officer's duty, especially at this season of the year.'

'But it must be done,' I suggested.

'Yes. But why not by native officers?'

'Would the treasure be safe with them?'

'Safe? Just as safe as it is now, if not safer; for, although I am responsible for the money in these boxes, I don't know that the whole amount is here. I didn't count it; and, if there was any deficiency, I should say so. Now, a native officer would satisfy himself on the subject before he took charge. Don't you see?'

Here our conversation was interrupted by a havildar (native sergeant), who appeared at the door of the tent, saluted the Lieutenant, and uttered in a deep and solemn tone of voice the word Sahib!

'Well. What's the matter?' said the Lieutenant.

'Maun Singh Sipahee is very ill.'

'What ails him?'

'He has fever.'

'Then I will come and see him in one moment.' With these words the Lieutenant threw down his cards, and invited me to accompany him to the tent wherein the patient was lying.

Maun Singh Sipahee was a powerful Brahmin, who stood upwards of six feet two. He was a native of Oude, and had a very dark skin. When we entered the tent, he attempted to rise from the charpai (native bedstead) on which he was reclining; but the Lieutenant told him to be still, then felt the sick man's pulse, and placed his small white hand across the broad black forehead of the soldier.

'Carry him into my tent. The ground is too damp for him here,' said the Lieutenant; and forthwith the bedstead was raised by half-a-dozen of the man's comrades. In the tent medicine was administered—a small quantity of tartar emetic dissolved in water, and given in very small doses, until nausea was produced, and a gentle perspiration stood upon the skin of the patient.

'You are all right, now, Maun Singh,' said the Lieutenant.

'No, Sahib, I am dying. Nothing can save me.'

'Then you know better than I do?'

'Forgive me, Sahib.'

'Listen. Lie very quiet; and, before we march, I will give you another sort of medicine that will set you up.'

The Sepoy covered his head over with his resaiee (counterpane), and lay as still as possible.

'They always fancy they are going to die, if there is anything the matter with them,' said the Lieutenant to me. 'I have cured hundreds of fever cases by this treatment. The only medicines I ever use in fever, sir, are tartar emetic and quinine. He has taken the one, which has had its effect; the other he shall have by and bye. I wouldn't lose that man on any account. His death would occasion me the greatest grief.'

'Is he a great favourite?' I asked.

'Not more than any of the rest of them who were with the regiment at Affghanistan, where they not only proved themselves as brave as the European soldiers, but where they showed themselves superior to prejudices most intimately connected with their religion—their caste. That man, whom you see lying there, is a Brahmin of the highest caste; yet, I have seen him, and other Brahmins now in my regiment, bearing upon their shoulders the remains of an officer to the grave. Of course, you are aware that to do a thing of that kind—to touch the corpse of an unbeliever—involves a loss of caste?'

'Yes.'

'Well, sir, these fellows braved the opinion and the taunts of every Hindoo in the country, in order to pay respect to the memory of those officers whose dangers and privations they had cheerfully shared. You are aware, perhaps, that at last the government found it necessary to issue a general order to the effect that any Sepoy of any other regiment who insulted the men of this regiment, by telling them they had lost their caste, would be severely punished and dismissed the service? Such was the case, sir; and many courts-martial were held in various stations for the trial of offenders against this order; and many Hindoo Sepoys and Mussulman native officers were very severely dealt with. And the thing was put down, sir; and now-a-days there is nothing more common than for the Hindoo Sepoys, in all the regiments, to ask permission to carry the remains of a popular officer to the grave. Indeed, ladies are often thus honoured, and children. They seem to have agreed amongst themselves that this does not involve a loss of caste. So much for caste, if it can be got over by an understanding amongst themselves! Caste! More than four-fifths of what they talk about it is pure nonsense and falsehood, as any straightforward native will confidentially confess to you. I don't mean to say that some Hindoos are not very strict. Many, indeed, are so. But I mean to say that a very small proportion live in accordance with the Shasters, and that when they cry out, 'if we do so and so we shall lose our caste,' it is nothing more than a rotten pretext for escaping some duty, or for refusing to obey a distasteful order. There are hypocrites in all countries, but India swarms with them more thickly than any country in the world. And the fact is that we foster hypocrisy. Our fellows, and most of them Brahmins, released a good many cats from the bag, when they were taunted with having lost their caste! If you are not in a frightful hurry to get on, stay till we march, and go with us; and I'll tell you and show you something more about caste. You can send on your palkee and bearers to the next encampment ground, and I'll drive you in my old trap of a buggy. It is not a remarkably elegant affair, but it is very strong and roomy. By the bye, we shall have to travel 'three in a gig;' for I must put Maun Singh, my sick Sepoy, between us; and you will find him a very intelligent fellow, I can tell you, and the dose I intend giving him will make him as chirpy as possible.'

The conversation and the manners of the Lieutenant—free and easy as were the latter—had fascinated me, and I accepted his invitation.

Marching

THE SMALL BUT heavy boxes containing the rupees were placed upon the hackeries (native carts), and the treasure party was now ready to march to the next encampment. The night was warm, and the Sepoys in what might strictly be termed half-dress. They wore their red cloth coats and their chacos; but their lower clothing was purely native; a dhotee (narrow strip of thick calico) wound round their loins, and falling in graceful folds about and below the knees. Some sat upon the boxes of treasure: others, not in line or military order, walked by the side thereof. The Lieutenant, Maun Singh, and myself brought up the rear. A syce (native groom) led the horse, and thus saved the Lieutenant the trouble of driving. The buggy was not, certainly, a very elegant affair. It was of very ancient construction, and the lining was entirely worn out; nor had the panels been painted for some years. The Lieutenant told me that he had bought this vehicle at a sale, five years previously, for the sum of five pounds, and that since that time it had travelled (marched, was the word he used) all over Bengal. The harness was of Cawnpore make; and, when new, had cost only two pounds ten shillings. Cawnpore, until recently, was chiefly famous for its harness, boots and shoes, bottle-covers, cheroot-cases, helmets, and other articles made of leather. A nest of Chinese settled in the bazaar many years ago and introduced the manufacture of such matters. The horse which drew the buggy had been a caster; that is to say, a horse considered no longer fit for the cavalry or horse artillery, and sold by public auction, after being branded with the letter R (signifying rejected) on the near shoulder. He was a tall, well-bred animal; and, according to the Lieutenant's account, had won no end of races since the day he had been knocked down to the Lieutenant for sixteen rupees, or one pound twelve shillings. The fault, or rather the misfortune, for which this animal had been dismissed the Company's service, was total blindness of one eye, and an inability to see much out of the other.

'But, he is a ripper, nevertheless,' said the Lieutenant, touching the animal very gently with the whip, and making him hold his head up; 'and will put some more money in my pocket next cold weather, I hope. He is entered for the Merchant's Plate, gentlemen riders, sir, and I am his jockey.' I expressed a hope that he would be successful.

It was a moonlight night, and slow as was the pace at which we proceeded, I never so much enjoyed a ride in my life. The scene altogether was highly picturesque, and, as far as I was concerned, had the wonderful charm of novelty; while it was impossible not to be extremely entertained by the volubility and lightheartedness of my military friend, who, notwithstanding he had extracted from me that I did not belong to the civil service or the army, had refrained from inquiring my name or pursuit, and invariably addressed me as Old Boy, albeit my years were certainly not in excess of his own.

'Well, Maun Singh!' cried the Lieutenant, 'how do you feel now?'

'Quite well, but very weak,' was the Sepoy's reply.

'Then you must have a little drop of weak brandy-and-water. Hold hard, syce, and give me the suraiee (water-bottle).'

The brandy-and-water was mixed in a silver tumbler, and handed to Maun Singh, who, as soon as the groom went again to the horse's head, applied it to his lips, and drank, without any scruple. On the contrary, it struck me that he liked the liquor.

'You have lost your caste,' said the Lieutenant, jocularly. 'You ought to have drunk it, you know, as medicine, out of your own lota (brass vessel).'

This observation—made with a view to draw the Sepoy out for my edification—had its effect. It was thus Maun Singh discoursed, while the Lieutenant and myself smoked our cheroots on either side of him:—

'The Sahib logue believe everything that the natives tell them about caste, and the consequence is they believe a great many falsehoods. If I could lose my caste by drinking medicine out of this tumbler, I would lose it by drinking it out of my own cup, because it came out of a bottle which you have handled, and perhaps some drops of it touched your fingers, while you were pouring it from one vessel to the other. Empty a bottle of brandy or gin into your chillumchee (brass wash-hand basin), and tell one of your palkee-bearers to throw it away. He and his companions will drink it, but not in your presence. Ask the same man to drink the liquor from your tumbler. He will put his hands together, and implore you to excuse him, as he would lose his caste.'

'But is it not forbidden in the Shasters?' said I.

'There is no mention of brandy in the Shasters, Sahib,' returned Maun Singh, with some humour. 'The Shasters are silent on the subject. But, supposing that it were forbidden; do not men of every religion frequently and continually depart from the tenets thereof, in minor things, or construe them according to their own inclination or convenience, or make some sort of bundobust (agreement) with their consciences? Indeed, if we did not make this bundobust, what Hindoo or Mussulman would come in contact at all with one another, or with Christians, and certainly we, the natives of India, would not serve as soldiers.'

'How so?'

'Because we should be in continual dread of having our bodies contaminated and our souls placed beyond the reach of redemption—and who would submit to that for so many rupees a month? Who can say what animal supplies the skin which is used for our chacos and accoutrements? The cow, or the pig? The Mussulmans, when we laugh together about it, say the cow. We protest that it is pigskin.'

'And how do you usually settle these disputes?' I inquired, with an eagerness which seemed to amuse the Sepoy.

'O, Sahib!' he replied, 'it would be a pity to settle any dispute of that kind, since it always affords us some merriment on a long march. When Pertab Singh came down to

Barruckpore to corrupt the regiments of native infantry there stationed, in eighteen hundred and forty-eight, he wanted them to protest against wearing the chacos.'

'And how was he received?' I inquired.

'They listened to him as long as his money lasted, and then made known to their officers what he was about.'

'And who was Pertab Singh?'

'A relation of the Ranee of Lahore.'

'And had he money?'

'Yes; and distributed freely.'

Here the Lieutenant informed me of the particulars relating to the mission of Pertab Singh, which was simply to excite the native troops to mutiny and to kill their officers; but the plot was happily discovered by the information given by the Sepoys of the 16th Grenadiers. 'There was an investigation, but the government deemed it best to treat the whole affair as a farce, and Pertab Singh was looked upon as a fool and a madman, and eventually set at liberty. It was said that the Sepoys who gave the information were to receive an order of merit; they had no reward at all, however, beyond some expressions of praise from the authorities.'

Suddenly, the treasure party halted, and all the Sepoys were speedily congregated beneath a mango tree.

'What is the matter?' cried the Lieutenant.

'Adjutant Bargow Sahib's grave,' said Maun Singh. 'Do you not remember the spot?'

'I did not, in this light,' said the Lieutenant, alighting from the buggy, followed by myself and Maun Singh. 'Yes; here he rests, poor fellow—one of the best and bravest beings that ever breathed. He died suddenly one morning when we were encamped here. He was a great favourite with the men, as you may judge from the respect paid by those now present to the spot where his ashes repose.'

One of the Sepoys suddenly began to call down curses on the head of some sacrilegious thief. He had discovered that the piece of marble which had been let into the head of the chunam (plaster) tomb, and on which was cut the name, age, and regiment of the deceased, had been abstracted.

'Ah! that of course,' said the Lieutenant. 'It is always the case. They steal the bit of marble to make a currystone—a stone on which they grind the ingredients for a curry. It was not worth more than a shilling, intrinsically; but if it had only been worth one anna, or a quarter of an anna—half a farthing—they would have carried it away all the same, just as they steal pieces of iron and lead from the stone bridges, and thus do immense mischief. All along the Grand Trunk Road you will find the stones used for headstones carried away from the graves.'

The march, thirteen miles, occupied us five hours, so slowly did the bullocks crawl along with the treasure. It was about four o'clock when we came to the ground—the hour at which, in strictness, the Lieutenant should have started; but he informed me that when on separate duty, he took a good deal of responsibility on himself, and without detriment to the interests of government, suited his own convenience and that of his men. He therefore preferred making night work of the business, and having the whole day at his own disposal.

'Send your bearers away, and spend the day with me,' said

the lighthearted Lieutenant. 'You can get other bearers at any of the villages in the neighbourhood; or, if you are not in a violent hurry, march the whole distance to Agra with me. I can stick your palkee and boxes on the top of the treasure, you know.'

I accepted the invitation with pleasure, and entered the tent, where we found tea and biscuits ready. After partaking of this refreshment we threw ourselves down on charpoys (native bedsteads), and soon fell fast asleep.

We slept till ten, when we arose, had breakfast, consisting of—the old story—grilled fowl, curried fowl, and eggs, with beer instead of tea; and then we went out and sat under the mango trees, which formed a dense shade over the encampment. The Lieutenant had with him a pellet bow, and was shooting at the squirrels which abound in the Upper Provinces of India. While he was thus employed a Sepoy—a Brahmin—called out: 'Sahib, you have no right to do that. It is written in the general orders that you must respect the religious feelings of the Hindoos, and here are you wantonly destroying the life of animals in our presence. I shall report this to the Colonel Sahib, when we return to the regiment.'

From the tone in which the Sepoy spoke, I thought he was in earnest. The Lieutenant, however, assured me that he was only ridiculing one of those absurd general orders which frequently appear, but of which bad and discontented Sepoys often take advantage. Ere long this Brahmin, observing that the light of the Lieutenant's cheroot was extinguished, brought him some fire. The Lieutenant gravely shook his head, and said—'No; it is written in general orders that no officer shall employ for his own purposes a Sepoy who is a soldier and not a servant, and that any officer so offending will subject himself to be tried by a court martial.' Then, taking the fire from the hand of the Brahmin, he remarked to me—'The consequence of that order, for which there never was the slightest occasion, is simply this: those men who are willing to oblige their officers laugh at it, while the disaffected will insolently quote it if required only to pick up a glove or a walking-stick. Many an officer has been severely reprimanded for asking a Sepoy to carry a letter for him to the post office.'

It was a very pretty scene, that encampment. The tents; the arms piled in front of them; the horse under a tree, and his syce seated near him; the old buggy and harness not far off; the Sepoys in groups employed in cooking their food for the mid-day meal; the numbers of brass vessels lying about in all directions; the score of squirrels hopping from branch to branch, or running up and down the trunks of the trees; the crows, the minars, and the sparrows on the look out for crumbs; the bullocks taking their rest after the fatigues of the past night; and then, before as well as after the meal, the men crowding round the well, and washing themselves from head to foot, and washing also their under garments, which are speedily dried in the sun of that climate. It is impossible to witness and not admire this part of the Hindoo and Mussulman religions.

After one o'clock, when every man had enjoyed his smoke, there was scarcely a soul, except myself and the Lieutenant, awake in the encampment. All were fast asleep in the open air. The Asiatic must sleep after his mid-day meal, if it be only for half an hour. The loss of this little sleep is a very severe privation.

At three o'clock the encampment was again all life. Some of the Sepoys wrestled, and exhibited amazing skill and strength in the art. To an European it is a mystery how men who live upon nothing but farinaceous food can be so muscular and powerful. Others smoked their pipes (small hookahs), and played at a native game called puchesee, resembling lotto; while a goodly number congregated around a Mussulman, who was reading aloud the *Bagh-o-Bahar*, a Hindoostanee work of great celebrity. Two or three of the company were musical, and played alternately on the sitarre (native guitar or violin), accompanied by the tom-tom (native drum), and the voices of those who were disposed and able to sing. As for the Lieutenant and myself we beguiled the time in conversation and with *écarté*. Towards sunset a palkee dâk carriage was reported to be in sight, coming down the road. 'Hooray!' cried the Lieutenant; 'come along! let us board him. I am in want of a few small matters.'

It was not long before the dâk carriage was abreast of the encampment.

'Stop!' shouted the Lieutenant to the driver, who instantly pulled up. 'Whom have you got inside?'

Before the driver had time to reply, the door was slided open, and an elderly gentleman, rubbing his eyes with his knuckles, put out his night-capped head, and exclaimed:

'Hulloa!'

'What! have we woke you out of your sleep, old boy?' said the Lieutenant, laughing.

'Yes,' replied the old boy, very good-humouredly, 'what do you want?'

'Only to ask you how you are.'

'I'm pretty well,' was the reply, 'but half choked with the dust.'

'What's taking you down the country?'

'Urgent private affairs.'

'Going to be married, I suppose?'

'Well, you have just guessed it.'

'Make my most respectful salaam to your intended, will you?'

'By all means.'

'When do you expect to reach Cawnpore?'

'To-morrow, at three p.m.'

'And how do you stand affected for liquors and weeds? Do you want anything, old boy? Brandy, beer, soda-water? Say the word.'

'Nothing; I have more in the well here than I shall be able to consume.'

'Then I'll trouble you for the surplus; for I am very short, and cannot get anything till I reach Agra, while you can replenish at every station, you know.'

'All right, my child,' exclaimed the old boy; and, with the greatest cheerfulness, he alighted and began to unpack his stores. From these, the Lieutenant took six bottles of beer, two bottles of brandy, a dozen of soda-water, and three hundred Manilla cheroots. This done, the old boy expressed a desire to push on; but the Lieutenant detained him for at least ten minutes with a series of questions, several of which

(I thought), were somewhat impertinent; for instance, he inquired his intended's name? whether she was tall, short, or of the middle height? what was the colour of her hair and eyes? good-looking, and accomplished? And to all these questions, the old boy responded with as serious an air as if the Lieutenant had a perfect right to put them.

At last the old boy proceeded on his journey.

'Do you know him?' I inquired of the Lieutenant, as the carriage rolled away.

'Oh, yes,' was the reply; 'he is a Major commanding a native infantry regiment at Banda. He is a very good fellow, and has heaps of property; but a frightful fool, except in the way of money-making, and at that he is awfully clever. I first made hisacquaintance in Affghanistan. He was then in the commissariat department, and was only taken out of that department about a year ago, when he attained his majority. He knows nothing whatever of soldiering, having been in staff employ ever since he was an ensign. All the Sepoys, as well as his officers, laugh *at* him as he comes on the parade ground and attempts to handle the regiment; and, after the farce is over, he laughs *with* them. For thirty years he was employed in commissariat duties, in which he is very efficient. At the expiration of that period, he became a Major; and then, according to the rules of the service, he was withdrawn from staff employ, and appointed to command a corps!'

'Surely you are jesting?'

'On my honour, I am serious. That is a part of our military system, sir.'

Here our conversation was interrupted by the approach

of the Soubadhar—native commissioned officer—who pronounced in a deep, sonorous, but feeble and inarticulate voice, that familiar word 'Sahib!' or, as more commonly pronounced, 'Sarb!'

'Well, old man, what is the matter?' said the Lieutenant to the almost imbecile native veteran, who had served in the time of Lord Lake, and who ought to have been pensioned many years previously, despite any remonstrances against such a measure. The old man forthwith began to detail a string of grievances, which the Lieutenant faithfully (?) promised to see remedied, albeit he could understand but a few words the old man said—so very indistinct was his speech, from sheer old age, and the loss of his teeth.

'A grievance, real or imaginary, is quite necessary for that old man's existence,' said the Lieutenant; 'and if he can't find one for himself (which is a very rare circumstance), he will concoct one for the Sepoys. To make grievances is the end and object of that old man's life; and, I am sorry to say, that he is a perfect representative of the entire body of native commissioned officers, who are, generally speaking, despised by the men of the regiment, as well as by the European officers. These are the gentlemen who brew or ferment all the mischief that occasionally occurs in native regiments. They suggest to the men to make all sorts of extortionate demands, just as a regiment is on the point of marching. That old man's present grievance, as far as I could collect, is that the water is very bad here, at this encampment ground, and that government ought to have a new well sunk. He happens just now to be suffering severely from one of the very many ailments consequent on his time of life, and he attributes it to the water.'

'Which happens to be very good,' I remarked.

'Precisely so. These native officers, of every rank and grade, are, in my opinion, the curse of the native service. Many very clear-headed and experienced officers have recommended doing away with them, and appointing in their stead more European officers; but the advice has never been heeded, and never will be, I fear.'

It was not until midnight that the little camp was broken up, and we resumed the march towards Agra. During the drive, the Lieutenant entertained me by relating a number of stories connected with the war in Affghanistan. Several of them interested me exceedingly; one, in particular. It was this; which I now give in the Lieutenant's own words, as nearly as I can recollect them.

'About a year ago,' said he, 'I was passing through Meerut, on my way from the Hills, whither I had been on sick certificate, and was putting up for a few days with my friend Richards, of the Light Cavalry—a man whom I had known during that disastrous campaign to which this narrative has reference. One morning, after breakfast, there came to the bungalow of my friend an Affghan, who was a dealer in dried fruits—such as grapes, apples, and pomegranates,—and inquired if the Sahib or mem Sahib was in want of any of these commodities, which he had just brought from Caubul. My friend's wife, who had also been in Affghanistan, and spoke the mongrel Persian current in that country, replied in the affirmative, and the Affghan was admitted to the verandah to exhibit his specimens and declare his prices. To talk to these dealers is rather amusing at times, especially when you know their habits, and customs, and peculiarities, as well as their language. To people who have been in their country, it is like meeting with an old friend, and one lingers as long as possible over the business of the bargain and sale. And so was it this morning. We had him for at least an hour in the verandah before my friend's wife would decide upon what she would take. This matter concluded, the Affghan inquired if the lady would buy a kitten—a Persian kitten; kittens being also a commodity with these travelling Affghans.

'Yes; where are the kittens?' said the lady.

'Here,' said the merchant, putting his hand into a huge pocket at the back of his chogah (a sort of gaberdine), and withdrawing, one by one, no less than sixteen of these little animals (all males). For more than the hour which was consumed in negotiating about the fruit, and talking on other subjects, this living bustle had remained perfectly motionless, and had not uttered a single sound; but now, when they saw the light, and were placed upon all-fours, they ran about and mewed—bushy tails on end—after the most vigorous fashion imaginable. There they were! Kittens as black as the blackest ink, kittens white as the whitest snow, kittens as yellow as the yellowest gold, and kittens piebald, brindled, and grey.

'There, mem Sahib; take your choice. Twenty rupees (two pounds) each.'

'The lady selected one of the white and one of the black kittens, and for the two he was induced to accept thirty-five rupees (three pounds ten shillings).

This may seem a large sum of money to give for a brace of young cats; but it must be remembered that they came from Bokhara, and were of the purest breed that could possibly be procured.

'The Affghan dealer took his leave, and promised to send the fruits in the course of the day. He fulfilled his promise; at tiffin-time there came a boy of about eleven years of age, bearing the basket containing them upon his head, which was shawled after the fashion of the Affghan people. The boy was admitted to the room. No sooner was he shown in, than his exceedingly beautiful countenance, and its peculiar expression, riveted the attention of all of us, and we put to him a variety of questions which he answered with great intelligence, and in a tone of voice so soft and silvery that even the guttural sounds he uttered came like music on the ear.

'Look into that boy's face,' said the lady to her husband and myself; 'observe his every feature, and his teeth,—regard especially his smile,—yes, and even the shape of his fingers, and then tell me of whom he is the very image.'

'I know,' said my friend.

'So do I,' exclaimed your humble servant.

'Stay!' said the lady, energetically. 'Do not speak; but let each of us write the name on a slip of paper, and see if we agree;' and tearing up an envelope and taking a tiny pencil-case from her watch-chain, she wrote a name upon one slip, and then handed to me and to her husband, respectively, a slip and the pencil-case. When we had each written a name, we compared them,—and they did not agree exactly. My friend and his wife had written Captain Percy ———, and I had written Mrs. Percy ———. That the boy was the offspring of that unfortunate couple (cousins), who perished in that campaign, and of whose young child no one ever knew what had become, we were all quite satisfied; and our reflections became extremely melancholy.

'We questioned the boy as to his parentage, his relation to the Affghan dealer in cats and fruit, and on a variety of other matters. His replies were simply to the effect that he was an orphan and a slave; that he knew not the place of his birth, but believed it was Affghanistan; that he was a Mahommedan, and that his earliest recollections were associated with Caubul.

'Whilst we were thus interrogating the boy, the Major of my friend's regiment, accompanied by his wife, drove up to the door. They had come to pay a visit. When asked to look at the boy, and say to whom he bore a resemblance, they at once declared, 'Poor Percy ———!' Several officers of the regiment were sent for. They came, and immediately on seeing the boy expressed an opinion that he was the child of the unfortunate officer whose name has been partially recorded. The poor boy, meanwhile, exhibited some anxiety to return to his master. Buthe was detained and further questioned as to the manner in which he was treated. He confessed that his master was rather severe, but withal a very good man.

'It was resolved to summon the Affghan dealer and make him render an account of the boy, and of how he became possessed of him. For this purpose a messenger was dispatched, and enjoined to make haste.

'The Affghan dealer came, and was cautioned that he must speak the truth; whereupon—as is the custom in India from one end to the other—he declared that he never spoke falsely, and that he would rather have his tongue torn out. This little preliminary over, the examination (which was conducted by the Major of the regiment, a very shrewd and clever man, and who, by the way, was distantly related to the unfortunate couple to whom the boy bore such a strong resemblance) commenced:—

'Who is this boy?'
'He belongs to me.'
'Your son?'
'No.'
'Any relation of yours?'
'No.'
'Your slave?'
'Yes.'
'You bought him?'
'Yes.'
'Where?'
'Caubul.'
'When?'
'Four years ago.'
'From whom did you buy him?'
'A merchant.'
'His name?'
'Usuf Ooddeen.'
'What did you give for him?'
'Three camels.'

'Of what value?'
'Thirty rupees (3*l.*) each.'
'The boy was cheap, then?'
'No.'
'How so?'
'He was young and sickly.'
'Did Usuf say where he got him from?'
'Yes.'
'Then tell me.'
'From a woman.'
'What woman?'
'A native of Hindostan.'
'An ayah?'
'Yes.'
'Was she his mother?'
'No.'
'Is she living?'
'No.'
'When did she die?'
'Eight years ago.'
'Where?'
'In Caubul.'
'Now tell us all you know about this boy.'
'I have answered all the Sahib's questions; will the Sahib answer a few of mine?'
'Yes.'
'Do you believe this boy to be of European birth?'
'Yes.'
'Do you think you know who were his parents?'

'Yes.'

'Were they people of a distinguished family?'

'Yes.' (This question was answered rather proudly.)

'Of pure blood?'

'Yes.'

'But is the Sahib certain that this boy is the child of certain parents?'

'Yes.'

'Then will the Sahib take him?'

'Yes.'

'Here the poor boy placed his hands together and supplicated the Major to let him remain where he then was, in the service of the Affghan dealer. Heedless of this interruption, which was soon silenced, the examination—or rather the conversation, as it now became—was continued:—

'What will you give for him?'

'What do you ask?'

'*You* must speak, Sahib.'

'One hundred rupees.'

'He cost me nearly that when he was very young and sickly.'

'Well, two hundred rupees.'

'No; Sahib. Half a lac of rupees would not purchase him.'

'But, my good man, slavery is not permitted in the British dominions, and we will detain the boy.'

'Against his will?'

'Yes.'

'On suspicion that he is born of European parents of distinction?'

'Yes.'

'Then I will give the boy his liberty; and if he then wishes to follow me, and you detain him, he is your prisoner instead of my slave.'

'Here the boy again entreated the Major to spare him.

'Never mind that.'

'But suppose that I could prove to you that he is the child of a sergeant of the Queen's 13th Regiment of Foot, and of his wife? What then? Would you take the boy?'

'Yes.'

'You would?'

'Yes.'

'Then you shall have the boy. Many of your questions I answered falsely, on purpose. The true history of the child I will recount to you, and produce such proofs as I have in my possession. I vowed to God and to the Prophet that I would never sell the child, and I have kept my word. It will be a bitter grief to me to part with him; but, for his own sake, I will endure it.

'Usuf Ooddeen was my elder brother. He kept a shop in the bazaar at Caubul. This child was brought to him by a woman of Hindostan, who not only deposited with him the child, but a sum of money in gold mohurs and rupees; likewise a quantity of English jewellery, and her own gold and silver bangles. She represented to my brother that the child's parents had been killed, and that she was afraid every European in Affghanistan would share their fate. My brother knew the woman, that is to say, she had been a customer at his shop, and had purchased from him sundry articles of warm clothing for her employers and herself. After leaving the child, and the money, and the jewellery, in all to the value of about four thousand rupees, she went her way, and never returned. It is most likely that she died suddenly of cold, like very many of the native servants of Hindostan, both male and female. The frost settled about their hearts, and they slept their lives away; or, if they escaped death, they lost their toes, fingers, ears, or noses.

'When the British army was victorious, and affairs were in a somewhat settled state, my brother was most anxious to deliver up the child, the money, and the jewels, to the British authorities; but a number of his friends dissuaded him from so doing, on the ground that the bare possession of the child would place my brother's life in jeopardy, by inducing a conclusion that he was the affrighted accomplice of murderers, assassins, and thieves. I confess that I was one who entertained this opinion, and I shook my head whenever my brother repeated his desire. Four or five years ago, my brother died, and I, a wandering dealer, became the guardian of this boy (for whom I have a great affection), and the holder of his money, for which I care not, and which I have no desire to retain. He has travelled thousands and thousands of miles with me. He has been to Bokhara, to Cashmere, all over the Punjab, to Mooltan, Scinde, all through the north-west provinces down to Calcutta, to Simlah, Mussooree—wherever the English have settled themselves in India; and I have done all in my power to expose him, in a quiet way, to the gaze of ladies and gentlemen, in the hope that some day he would be recognised and restored to his proper position in life. Never, until now, has any one been struck with his countenance, beyond casually remarking to me that he was a very pretty boy; certainly, no one ever seemed to have the slightest idea that he was born of European parents, and is a Christian; for he is not a Mussulman—though he thinks he is a Mussulman, and says his prayers, and is very constant to all the observances of the Mussulman faith. Gentleman, I am a wandering dealer from Affghanistan, but I am not destitute of good feeling and integrity, little as you may credit my assertions in this respect. Give me a proof that you know who were the child's parents, and I am willing to restore him, and all that rightfully belongs to him, to your custody.'

'But are you not satisfied with my word? Never mind the money and the jewels—much as I should like to see the latter—all I require is the boy,' said the Major.

'Of course, the Sahib would not speak an untruth knowingly,' returned the Affghan. 'But I require some proof that the boy is the child of certain European parents.'

'Well, there is the likeness, the unmistakeable likeness, that he bears to his father and his mother.'

'That will not do,' said the Affghan, interrupting the Major. 'Can you write in the Persian character, Sahib?'

'Yes.'

'Then, write the name of this boy's father in the Persian character, and let me see it.'

The Major did this, and handed it to the Affghan, who looked at the writing, smiled, and said:

'What else? What was the Sahib's nishan (crest)?'

'This,' said the Major, holding out the littlefinger of his

right hand, upon which was a signet-ring. 'This was his nishan. We are of the same family, and the nishan is the same.'

'The Affghan, having examined the crest, again smiled, and said:—

'What else?'

'What more do you want?' said the Major.

'Do not be impatient, Sahib,' said the Affghan. 'The identification of a child, who may be an heir to property, is not so light a matter as the purchase of a kitten. Did you know the child's mother?'

'Yes,' said the Major. 'She was also a relation of mine.'

'What kind of person was she? Was she handsome?'

'Very.'

'The colour of her eyes?'

'Dark—almost black.'

'And her hair?'

'Brown; the colour of this lady's' (pointing to the wife of my friend).

'If you saw her likeness, in miniature, do you think you could recognise it?'

'If it were a faithful likeness, I could.'

'The Affghan put his hand into the breast pocket of his chogah, and produced a greasy leathern bag, into the mouth of which he inserted his finger and thumb, and presently produced a small tin box, round and shallow, which he very carefully opened.

Having removed some cotton, he handed the box to the Major. All of us instantly recognised the features of the unfortunate lady who had perished by the side of her husband, in Affghanistan. Who could possibly forget that sweet feminine face of hers, which had been painted for her husband by one of the most distinguished miniature painters of the age? The production of the likeness in the presence of the boy (who appeared to take little interest in what was going on), had a sad effect upon the Major. He sat down upon a chair, covered his manly face with his hands, and wept bitterly.

'And do you know this, Sahib?' asked the Affghan, when the Major had somewhat recovered his violent emotion: placing in his hand poor Percy's seal.

'We all recognised the seal, the crest of which, of course, corresponded with the crest on the signet-ring of the Major.

'And this?' asked the Affghan, holding up a bracelet which we had seen Mrs. Percy wear many and many a time.

'And this?' holding up to our gaze a small brooch she used to wear constantly. And, amongst numerous other things, he exhibited to us a little pocket-book, in which she kept her memoranda, such as:—'November 9th. Cut the ends of my dear little boy's hair. Sent mamma a small portion.— November 12th. Had a long talk to the old ayah, who swore to me that she would ... and I believe her, for she has been a good and constant creature to us, in our dangers and our difficulties.'

'And this? And this? And this? And this?' said the Affghan, withdrawing from the leathern bag its entire contents, every article of which was instantly identified. 'There, Sahib, take them all, and the boy, into your custody. The money, which was left with him, I will restore to you to-night. It is at present in the bazaar, in the charge of my camel, whom no one dare approach, except myself and this boy.'

'Here a very extraordinary and painful, but perhaps natural, scene occurred. The boy, who had been comparatively passive, now broke out into a vehement expostulation, and spoke with a rapidity which was truly amazing, considering that he distinctly enunciated every syllable to which he gave utterance. 'What!' he exclaimed, 'will you then leave me in the hands and at the mercy of these unbelievers? What have I done to deserve this?'

'Be quiet,' said the Affghan to the boy, in a gentle tone of voice.

'How can I be quiet?' cried the boy, clenching his fists convulsively, and drawing himself up, whilst his eyes glared, and his nostrils dilated, with uncontrollable passion, and something like foam stood upon his crimson lips. There could be no doubt whose child he was, so wonderful in his wrath was the likeness that he bore to his father, who was very seldom provoked to anger, but who, when it did happen, was 'perplexed in the extreme:' in short, a perfect demon until the paroxysm was over.

'Baba (child)!' said the Major, 'listen to me.'

'Don't talk to him now, Sahib,' said the Affghan, compassionately. 'In his anger his senses always leave him, and he cannot hear what you say. Let him exhaust his fury upon me. He will be powerless presently.'

'And so it was. After a brief while, the boy sat down on the carpet, gasped for breath, and was seemingly unable to move or speak. The lady of the house offered him a glass of water, but he shrunk back, and declined to receive it from her hand.

'The Affghan took the Major aside, spoke to him in private, and then left the room. Here another very painful scene ensued. The boy, exhausted as he was, attempted to follow his late master; he was restrained, of course; whereupon he uttered the most heart-rending cries that ever were heard. The Major had him conveyed to his bungalow, where a room was set apart for him, and a servant and an orderly had him in their keeping. It was a month before the boy could be reconciled to his 'fate,' as he called it; and soon afterwards arrangements were made for sending him home to his grandfather and grandmother, who are persons of a lofty position in life and very wealthy. They received him with extreme affection, and on the death of his grandfather, he will succeed to a title and an estate worth eleven thousand a-year. The Affghan, who was very fond of the boy, corresponds with him regularly, and they exchange presents, as well as letters.

'Kelly, of the 62nd, who was killed at Ferozeshah, and who formerly belonged to the 13th Foot, when they were in Affghanistan, told me a more curious story of a little girl, than the one I have related to you of this boy.'

'What was it?' I asked.

'My dear fellow,' said the Lieutenant, 'I cannot talk any more just now. You shall have it some other day. We are not going to part company yet, old boy.' With these words he fell asleep, his feet over the dashboard, and his head resting on my shoulder.

The March Continued

THE NEXT ENCAMPMENT-GROUND at which we halted was close to a dâk bungalow; and, during the day, there were several arrivals and departures, the travellers merely halting for an hour or so, while some refreshment was got ready. The Lieutenant, who appeared to know everybody in Hindostan (I never met a person who did not know him), contrived, to use his own phrase, to 'screw a small chat out of each of them.' On one occasion he returned to the tent richer than he left it. He carried in one hand a small basket containing preserved oysters, crystallized apricots, and captains' biscuits, and in the other a stone bottle of Maraschino. Under his arm was a quantity of gauze, which he wanted for a veil, he said. These contributions he had levied from a lady who was going to Muttra, where her husband was an official of some magnitude. She had just returned from England, the Lieutenant informed me, and was looking as blooming as possible. To my question, 'Do you know her?' he responded, 'Oh yes; she is one of my sixty!'

'Sixty what?'
'First cousins.'
'All in India?'

'Every one of them. My good sir, I have at this moment, in the Bengal Presidency alone, upwards of two hundred and twenty relations and connexions, male and female, and every one of them—that is to say, the men and the boys—in the service of the government.'

'Is it possible?'

'Yes. What is more, four-fifths of the number are in the civil service. I should have been in the civil service too, only I was sent away from Haileybury for rebellion and card-playing. It is not an easy matter for me to go to any station in these provinces without finding a cousin in it.'

'Do you know the assistant-magistrate of Agra?'

'Yes.'

'Is he a cousin of yours?'

'*He* isn't. But his wife's father and my father were own brothers; so it amounts to pretty much the same thing.'

'And do you know the judge of Jampore?' This was a gentleman to whom I had letters of introduction.

'Yes. His mother was my aunt.'

'It must be dangerous,' I suggested, 'to express an opinion of any one in India in the presence of a man who has so very many relations.'

'Oh, dear no!' said the Lieutenant. 'A man with such a frightful lot of connexions has no right to be, and is not generally, very sensitive. Bless me! if I had nothing to do but to stand up for my relations, I should run the risk of being perpetually knocked down. Life is much too short for that sort of thing. Therefore, when I hear any one abuse or reflect upon any relation or connexion of mine, I am invariably silent; or, if appealed to, express my indifference by a shrug of the shoulders.'

Here we were interrupted by the old Soubahdar, who came to the door of the tent. He had dined, washed, smoked, slept, and had now got up to grumble. His huge teak-box, which measured four feet by two, and two feet deep, and without which he never travelled, had received a slight injury, and of this he had come to complain. He said, that in the time of Lord Clive or Lord Lake, if such a thing had happened, the men in charge of the hackeries (carts) would have been hanged on the spot; and Phool Singh Brahmin, whose exertions, he alleged, prevented the utter destruction of the box, would have been promoted to the rank of havildar.

'Clive and Lake!' whispered the Lieutenant to me. 'He talks like a leading article in a London newspaper.' Then, turning to the old man, he inquired, 'Would Lord Clive or Lord Lake have sanctioned your carrying about that beastly trunk on a march at all?'

'Yes, Sahib.'

'It is not true. Lord Clive and Lord Lake gained their victories by the help of self-denying men, who cheerfully endured any personal inconvenience; not by a parcel of old grumblers like yourself, who have no right to refer to the career of those illustrious men.'

'Sahib, I was with Lord Lake's army.'

'Then, that's the very reason that you ought not to be here.'

'But our present Colonel, Sahib, was with Lord Lake.'

'And I wish he was with Lord Lake now!'

'I shall report this, Sahib.'

'Very well. Do!'

Whereupon the old officer left the tent, and the Lieutenant assured me that the Colonel, who was as imbecile as the Soubahdar, would cause the matter to be investigated, and that he, the Lieutenant, would, to a certainty, receive a severe reprimand.

'For what?' I asked.

'For not having made arrangements for the safe conveyance of the baggage, and for having treated with a want of courtesy a native commissioned officer of the regiment. I need scarcely say, that this reprimand will not in any way interfere with my night's rest.'

'But, the complainant will forget it,' said I, 'before he gets back to the regiment.'

'Forget it!' exclaimed the Lieutenant. 'Forget it! A native—especially a native commissioned officer—forget a grievance! Catch that old man forgetting the slightest unpleasantness that has occurred to him during this march. He will, it is true, forget his present grievance to-morrow, when he has a fresh one; but at the end of the journey they will be forthcoming in a lump.'

This prophecy was destined not to be fulfilled; for, presently, a Sepoy came to the Lieutenant, and reported that the Soubahdar was very ill. We hastened to the old man's tent, and found him, strange to say, in the last extremity. He was going very fast; but, nevertheless, he continued to gurgle forth a grievance. He demanded, with his last breath—why the East India Company did not give him his pay, as in Lord Lake's time, in *sicca* rupees?

'You shall, in future, receive it in *sicca* rupees,' said the Lieutenant, bending over the old man, whose hand he grasped tightly.

'And will my losses be made good?' he asked, with awful energy.

'Yes,' said the Lieutenant.

'It is well!' and the old man slipped almost imperceptibly from one world to another.

That the old Soubahdar, who was upwards of eighty, had died of natural causes, there could be no question; but, clamorous as was the entire company for the interment of the body, the Lieutenant determined on taking it to Agra, for the purpose of a surgical examination. Meanwhile the old man's effects were scrupulously collected and put under seal.

We were now only twenty-six miles from Agra, the capital of the North West Provinces, and it was agreed to perform the distance in one march. We therefore started at sundown, and travelled all night. The moon was shining brightly, the road was in excellent order, and, notwithstanding that the old Soubahdar was lying lifeless on the top of some of the treasure-boxes, the Sepoys were in high spirits, and on several occasions even jocular in respect to the deceased's weakness—that of perpetually grumbling.

Shortly after the day had dawned, I beheld on the distant horizon something like a large white cloud. Had we been at sea, I should have said it was a sail or an iceberg, to which it bore a striking resemblance. I pointed it out to the Lieutenant, who smiled.

'Don't you know what that is?' he said.

'No,' I answered.
'Can't you guess?'
'No. What is it?'
'That is the famous Taj Mahal. That is the building that defies the most graphic pen in the world to do justice to its grandeur and its transcendent beauty. Bulwer, in the *Lady of Lyons*, has a passage which sometimes reminds me of the Taj:—

A palace lifting to eternal summer
Its marble halls from out a glassy bower
Of coolest foliage, musical with birds.

But how far short must any description of such aplace fall! How far distant do you suppose we are from that building?'
'About two miles.'
'Upwards of nine miles, as the crow flies! Yes; that is the Taj, the tomb of a woman, the wife of the Emperor Shah Jehan. The pure white marble of which it is built was brought from Ajmere. For upwards of twenty-five years, twenty-five thousand men were employed, day by day, on that edifice. I am afraid to say how many millions it cost. The Mahrattas carried away the huge silver gates and made them into rupees. What became of the inner gate, which was formed of a single piece of agate, no one can say. The general opinion is, that it is buried somewhere in Bhurtpore. The original idea was, to build a corresponding tomb on this side of the river for the Emperor himself, and connect the two by a bridge of white marble. A very pretty idea, was it not? Lord William Bentinck

was for pulling the Taj down and selling the marble, or using it for building purposes.'

'Impossible!'

'Not at all. He thought it was very impolitic to allow these gorgeous edifices to stand—these monuments of folly, extravagance, and superstition, which served none but the worst of prejudices, leading the natives to draw prejudicial comparisons between the simple and economical structures of the British and these stupendous and costly erections of the Moghul Emperors. And most assuredly our bungalows, churches, and other buildings do present a most beggarly appearance alongside these masses of polished marble and red stone. It looks as though we had no confidence in our hold of the country, and therefore would not go to any expense worth speaking of. Look at our court-houses, in the civil lines, as that part of Agra is called—a parcel of paltry brick and mortar pigeon-holes, not to be compared with the tenements that the menial servants of the Emperors inhabited. Look at the Government House, the Metcalfe Testimonial, and other paltry European edifices.'

'Surely,' said I, 'you would preserve rather than deface or destroy these magnificent works of art—these wonders of the world?'

'Works of art and wonders of the world they doubtless are; but, under existing circumstances, they are eye-sores, and I would pull down every one of them, and convert the material into useful buildings—barracks—splendid barracks for our British and native troops; hospitals, worthy of being called hospitals; court-houses, churches, magazines, and so forth.'

'But what barbarians the natives would think us!'

'What does that signify? Are we the conquerors of the country, or are we not? As to what they would think of us, they can't think much worse of us than they do already. Do we not eat swine's flesh? and do not English ladies dance (the natives call it 'jumping about'), and with men who are not their husbands? Barbarians! Why, the very dress that we wear renders us barbarians in their sight.'

The sun had now risen high in the heavens, and his rays fell upon the Taj, which we were gradually approaching. I was wrapped in admiration, and wishing in my inmost heart that my talkative companion would cease, and leave me to gaze in silence on that glorious scene, when suddenly the procession halted, and the Lieutenant shouted out the word 'Hulloa!' in a voice so loud that I was completely startled.

'What is the matter?' I asked.

'Matter!' the Lieutenant echoed me. 'Matter! Look a-head! There is a wheel off one of those rickety carts, and those confounded boxes are scattered all over the road.' Here the little officer bounded like an Indian-rubber ball from his seat, and in a towering passion with all the world in general, but no one in particular, rushed to the spot where the disaster had occurred, and there began to fret, fume, and snort most violently.

'Hush, Sahib!' said one of the Sepoys, saluting his officer very respectfully, 'or you may wake the Soubahdar, and *then* what will happen?'

This appeal had the effect of restoring the Lieutenant to calmness and good-humour. He smiled, and seemed to feel that matters would certainly have been worse, and the delay more protracted, had the old man been alive and witnessed the accident.

One of the boxes was smashed to pieces, and the rupees were lying about in all directions, the Sepoys picking them up, and searching for others in the dust and sand. I never witnessed a more ridiculous or grotesque scene than this—the native soldiers in their red coats and chacos, but with bare legs and without shoes, kneeling, and sifting the earth through their fingers, the Lieutenant in his pyjamahs and solar hat, a cheroot in his mouth, and in his hand the buggy-whip, which he used as a baton while giving his orders.

'Does this often happen?' I was tempted to ask.

'Constantly,' was the Lieutenant's reply. 'The Government has a bullock-train for the conveyance of stores; and even private individuals, by paying for the carriage, may have their goods taken from station to station; but, in respect to treasure, we cling to the old system. The military authorities apply to the magistrates, whose subordinates provide these hackeries, which were in vogue some five thousand years ago. And just observe those rotten boxes.'

'Why are they not lined with cast iron or zinc?'

'It would be too expensive. The Government cannot afford it.'

'But why should not the Government use its own bullock-train for the conveyance of treasure, instead of hiring these antiquated and rotten conveyances?'

'Because the bullock-train is under the post-office authorities; and the military authorities have nothing to do with the post-office authorities.'

'Is that a reason?'

'No—nor is it rhyme; but it is a part of our Indian system, and, what is more, it is Government logic. However, I am not going to stop here all day. We will push on, and get into Agra before breakfast. The treasure will come all right enough, and I will be there to meet it at the office of the magistrate and collector.'

We now took our seats in the old buggy. The hood was raised, the syce sat behind, and off we went at a canter, which very soon became a gallop. In the parlance of the Lieutenant, the old horse was indeed 'a ripper.' When warm there was no holding him, and he went over his seven and a half miles of ground in thirty-seven minutes. At the bridge of boats which crosses the Jumna, we met, by chance, the assistant magistrate (the friend with whom I was going to stay, and the husband of the Lieutenant's first cousin). He was dressed in a pair of large jack-boots, corduroy breeches, a shooting-coat, and a solar helmet, and was riding an immensely powerful Cape horse. He did not recognise either of us at first, but pulled up, and turned round the moment the Lieutenant shouted out his name, with the addition of 'Old boy!'—household words in the mouth of the Lieutenant, for he not only applied them to things animate, but inanimate; for instance, his corkscrew, his teapot, his buggy, his watch, his hat, everything with him was an old boy, in common with the Lieutenant-Governor, or the general commanding the division.

After I had been greeted by my friend, who had been at a loss to account for my delay in reaching Agra—the Lieutenant thus addressed him:

'I say, old boy. Look here. I have a lot of treasure for you about seven or eight miles from this; but there has been a break down. Send out a lot of fellows to give assistance, will you?'

'Yes.'

'And look here, old boy. There's a dead Soubahdar.'

'A what?'

'A dead Soubahdar. He died suddenly, and I don't wish him to be buried without an examination, because I bullied him mildly only a short time previous to his going out. You will manage that for me, old boy, won't you?'

'Oh, yes.'

'He died of old age, and his last grievance; but still I should like a medical man's certificate; just to satisfy the colonel who served with him in Lord Lake's time, you know, and all that sort of thing.'

'I can manage all that for you,' replied the official, riding by the side of the buggy; 'but push on, for the sun is becoming rather oppressive, and I have no hood to my saddle, remember.'

My host and hostess made me as comfortable and as happy as any traveller could wish to be made. Of the former I saw little or nothing from eleven in the morning till three or four in the evening, for he was what is called a conscientious officer, and attended strictly to his work. During these hours I used to read, or pay a visit to the mess-rooms of a regiment where a billiard-table was kept. To the officers of the regiment I was introduced by Lieutenant Sixtie, previous to his return to his own corps. He stayed eight days in Agra—upon some plea or other—and sent his company on, in advance of him.

Agra—that is to say, the society of Agra—was at the time split into two sections, the civil and the military. They were not exactly at open war, but there was a coolness existing between the two branches. They did not invite each other, and very seldom exchanged calls. For me, who was desirous of seeing all parties, this was rather awkward, living as I was in the house of a civilian. So I resolved upon taking a small bungalow for a short period, and furnishing it in a mild and inexpensive manner. I was candid enough to confess to my host that, as I was in no way connected with either branch of the service, I was anxious to avoid taking any part in their local differences; and he had the good sense not to press me to remain under his roof.

A few days after I had located myself in my bungalow, I received a call from a native gentleman, a Seik chieftain, who was, and now is, a state prisoner on a handsome stipend. He drove up to my door in a small phaeton, drawn by a pair of large black mules of incredible swiftness and agility. This fallen chieftain—a tall and powerfully-built man—was no other than the renowned Rajah Lall Singh, who commanded the Seik cavalry at the battle of Ferozeshah, and who was subsequently Prime Minister at Lahore, during a portion of the time that the British Government undertook the administration of the Punjab on behalf of Maharajah Dulleep Singh. Lall Singh was now studying surgery. More than one medical officer in charge of the hospitals which he attended, informed me that the Rajah was already a comparatively skilful operator, and could take off an arm or a leg with surprising dexterity. Notwithstanding his previous character—that of a sensualist and faithless intriguer; one, indeed, who had not been constant even to his own villanies— I could not help liking his conversation, which was humorously enlivened with imitations of English officers with whom he had come in contact, and was entertaining to the last degree. His anecdotes, relating to the late Runjeet Singh, were peculiarly interesting; coming as they did from the lips of a man who had been so much in the company of that remarkable monarch, who in many respects resembled Napoleon the First, especially in the selection of the instruments of his power. 'All his' (Runjeet's) 'chief men,' said the Rajah, 'were persons of obscure origin: Tej Singh, Sawan Mull, Deenanauth, and the rest of them.'

'But you were an exception,' said I.

'Indeed not,' was his reply. 'I began life as a muleteer, and hence my partiality for mules, perhaps.'

After a while the Rajah invited me to take a drive with him, to a house about two miles in the country, and situated on the banks of the Jumna. It was not his own house, which was then under repair, he said, but had been placed at his disposal by a friend. I thanked the Rajah, and stepped into his carriage; he followed me, seized the reins, shook the whip, and away we went at the rate of sixteen miles an hour.

The garden-house, at which we soon arrived, was a spacious building of European architecture. It had formerly belonged to a general officer who had married a native woman of considerable wealth. The furniture was all of European make, and was arranged very much in the same manner as that in the Sahib Logue's apartments at Bhitoor. In point of quality it was also very much the same—a portion costly, and the rest of a common description. This house, too, was constantly inhabited by English folks who sought a change of air for a few days. Since his removal to Agra, Lall Singh lived more like an European than a native, and had got into the habit of sitting at ease in a chair, instead of cross-legged like a tailor on the carpet. His dress was of the simplest and most unpretending character imaginable; and, with the exception of a signet-ring on his forefinger, he had no ornament on his person. The table of the apartment to which he conducted me was literally covered with surgical instruments—saws, knives, scalpels of every size and shape. Amongst them I perceived a pair of swords in wooden scabbards covered with rich green velvet, and ornamented with gold and precious stones. Observing that my eyes rested on these swords, he took one up, and remarked, 'These have performed some curious operations in their time; but never in a hospital. They have been used chiefly for taking off heads. This once belonged to Dhyan Singh, and that to Heera Singh, who were both assassinated. They are of Damascus steel, and are sharper than any of these knives or scalpels. I have sent a number of swords to England to have them made into surgical instruments.' Here our conversation was interrupted by a domestic, who announced—

'The Lallah Sahib;' and presently a native gentleman walked, or rather limped (for he was lame of the right leg) into the room, and made a very graceful salaam, first to the Rajah and then to myself. He was rather short in stature, but very stoutly built, and about forty years of age. His eyes were full of intelligence and vigour, and his features regular and well-shapen. His manners were easy, affable, unassuming, and modest, and his attire as plain and quiet as possible.

'This gentleman, Sahib,' said the Rajah, addressing me, 'is a great friend of mine. This house belongs to him. A strange world is this! Only a few years ago, I offered a reward of a lac of rupees (ten thousand pounds) for his head, or two lacs to any one who would bring him alive to my tent.'

'Indeed!'

'Yes; and if I had caught him, how changed would have been the whole face of affairs in this country!'

'How so?'

'This gentleman was the contractor for the British army; and, if I had got hold of him, the army could not have been supplied.'

'But why was he worth more alive than dead?' I asked, with a laugh, in which the native gentleman heartily joined.

'Because,' returned the Rajah, coolly, 'if we had secured him alive we would have made him feed us with the supplies bought with his own money; which should also have paid the reward for his capture. This, by the way, was claimed by several who brought in heads, alleging that each was the head of the Lallah the contractor; but the attempted imposition was discovered, and the perpetrators were themselves decapitated.'

Unlike Hindoos and Mussulmans, who drink in secret, Lall Singh drank neat brandy openly; and, rising from his chair, he administered unto himself a couple of glasses—or rather a tumbler half-filled—on this occasion. He could take more than two bottles of brandy without being in the least intoxicated. This was owing, of course, to the circumstance that he consumed considerable quantities of bhang; just in the same way that an opium-eater is rarely or never affected by drinking deeply of wine.

The Rajah's visitor, the Lallah Jooteepersad, had a grievance, and a rather substantial one. He had claimed from the Government fifty-seven lacs of rupees (half a million and seventy-thousand pounds sterling) as the balance due to him for feeding the armies employed during the two Seik campaigns; and the Government had threatened to prosecute him, in one of their own courts, for an attempt to make an overcharge of forty thousand rupees, or four thousand pounds.

'And if they understand the principles of good government thoroughly,' said the Rajah, 'they will convict you, imprison you for life, and confiscate all your possessions, real and personal. That is the way the Lahore Durbar would have settled so large a claim. But the Indian Government has not the courage to act in that way.'

'But I have not attempted to make an overcharge; and if my agents have done so, let it be deducted, if it be incorrect,' said the Lallah.

'You are a criminal,' said the Rajah.

'How so?' asked the Lallah.

'You say the Government owes you fifty-seven lacs?'

'Yes—and honestly.'

'Well, is not that enough to warrant your being transported for life, or hanged? But, as I have told you, the Government has not courage to prosecute you.'

In this opinion, however, Lall Singh was in error; for, that very night, the Lallah was informed that he was, to all intents and purposes, a prisoner, and must not leave Agra. The firm belief of every native, not only in the district but throughout India, was, that these proceedings had been taken to evade payment of the contractor's just demands. But the Lallah himself was the first to deny this assertion, and to declare that the prosecution arose out of the circumstance of the Commissary-General being a near relative of the Governor-General of India; that a civilian in power had a quarrel with the Commissary-General, and had represented, semi-officially, that great frauds had been committed, and there could be no question that the heads of the departments were cognisant of such frauds; that the Governor-General, anxious that the honour of a member of his ancient family should be cleared up, had determined upon a strict investigation; and that the civilian in question suggested the public prosecution of the contractor as the speediest and most satisfactory means of arriving at the result!

And such was the opinion of many officers of the Government, civil and military!

The contractor, however, was eventually acquitted, and the Government paid the bill. But, to this day, the natives of India believe that the object of the Government was to cheat their creditor; while the officers, civil and military, are equally sanguine that it was 'the honour of the family' that led to the most extraordinary and protracted trial that ever was known in India, and which was emphatically denounced, by the press and public; of every country in Europe, as absurd, unjust, and shameful. Nevertheless, Jooteepersâd cannot have harboured any revenge for the wrongs (involving disgrace and dishonour) which were heaped upon him; for it is he who has fed, for several months, the five thousand Christians during their incarceration in the fortress of Agra; and, amongst the number of civilians there shut up, is the gentleman who conducted the prosecution on the behalf of the Government, and who, in the execution of his duty, strove very hard indeed for a verdict of guilty! Without Jooteepersâd we could not have held Agra!

When the sun had gone down, and it was cool enough to walk abroad, Lall Singh led me into the extensive gardens which surrounded his temporary abode. The Lallah had left us, and I was now alone with the ex-Commander of the Seik Cavalry and the ex-Prime Minister of Lahore. I felt much more pleasure in his society than I should have felt had he been in the plenitude of his power; for he bore his altered condition with great dignity and cheerfulness, and discoursed upon all sorts of topics without any restraint or reserve. He even talked about the Ranee of Lahore—with whom his name had been so frequently coupled—and with a chivalrous spirit (whether his assertions were true or not is another matter) assured me that his intrigues with her had been confined exclusively to politics. I asked him where this helpless woman had fled to, after her miraculous escape from Benares, in the garb of a man? He replied that he knew not. He was sure she was not in Nepal—where the authorities supposed her to be—but somewhere in our own provinces.

'Was she a beautiful woman?' I asked.

'No; and never had been,' was his reply. 'But she had eyes which could charm like those of a snake, and a voice sweeter than that of a bird.'

'They say she was the Messalina of the East,' and I explained to him what the allusion signified.

'It is not true,' he exclaimed vehemently. 'She was a vain and clever woman; but the very opposite of the character that she has been described. She was proud of the influence she possessed over men in making them subservient to her will and her caprices.'

'Had she great power over Runjeet Singh?'

'None. She was his doll, his plaything, and the only being who could calm him when he had the horrors. Nothing more.'

'How the horrors?'

'Runjeet Singh began life as a petty chieftain, with a few hundred followers. He acquired a vast kingdom, and had the most powerful army that the East ever saw, or will see. Whilst he went on conquering, shedding blood, and plundering, he was easy in his mind; but, when he found that he had got as much as he could manage, he stopped; and then came his disquiet. His great fear then was that he could not retain what he had become possessed of—and his chief horror was that the Koh-i-noor would be carried off—that diamond which Runjeet Singh stole, and which the Ranee has worn a thousand times as a bracelet. That diamond which is now in the crown of England.'

'Where did it come from originally?'

'No one can say that. The history of the Koh-i-noor has

yet to be written. Did you ever see a likeness of Runjeet Singh?'

'Never.'

'Then I will show you a very faithful one; a miniature taken by a famous painter who came from Delhi, and spent his life in Lahore. The Maharajah was a diminutive, shrivelled man, frightfully pitted with the small-pox, which had destroyed one of his eyes; but with the other he could gaze for an hour without ever winking. He had a shrill and squeaking voice; but it terrified those who heard it, especially when he was angry. He did not talk much; but he was a great listener. Then, shrivelled and emaciated as he was in his later years, he was possessed of immense physical strength when roused; and upon horseback, where skill could be exercised, few men in his kingdom could have disarmed him.'

'Indeed!'

'He inspired all those who approached him—whether European or native—with respect mingled with intense fear.'

Our conversation was here interrupted by a gardener, who presented the Rajah and myself respectively with a nosegay; and who volunteered the information, that some workmen, in digging the foundation for a vine trellis had come upon an old house under the earth, and in it had been found several gold and silver coins.

'Where?' asked the Rajah.

'There,' said the gardener, pointing in the direction.

We hurried to the spot, and found that the workmen had gone; but sure enough, there were the walls of an apartment, formed of red stone and white marble.

'This quarter of Agra,' said the Rajah to me, 'was formerly inhabited by persons of the highest rank. Where we are now standing was, no doubt, once the site of a palace; and these walls are those of the ty-khana—a vault beneath the dwelling from which the light is excluded. In these dark places are usually perpetrated what you English call 'dark deeds.'

I expressed a desire to explore this newly discovered apartment of former days; but the Rajah told me it was then too late, as the workmen had gone; but he promised me that if I would come to him at daylight on the following morning, he would have great pleasure in gratifying my curiosity.

On the following morning, having spent a very dreamy night, I was carried in my palanquin to the Jatnee Bagh. Such was the name of Jooteepersâd's garden-house, in which Lall Singh then resided. The Rajah was dressing. I was confronted by a Seik with an enormous beard, whose hair was a yard long and tied up in a peculiar knot on the top of his head, and who politely inquired if I would take coffee. Ere long the Rajah made his appearance, and we went together to the newly discovered ty-khana, which was now guarded, since gold and silver had been found there. The workmen, some twenty in number, came and commenced their labour: that of clearing away the earth in all directions, in order to get to the bottom of the apartment in the ty-khana. This was accomplished in about two hours, and we then stood upon a stone-floor in the centre of a room, about sixteen feet square. In several of the niches were little lamps, such as are burnt upon the tombs of Moslems, and a hookah and a pair of marble chairs were found in the subterraneous apartment; of which the sky was now the roof. Whilst examining the walls, I observed that, upon one side, there was a ledge about six feet high from the floor (and carried up therefrom), and about a foot in width. This ledge, which was of brick and plaster, resembled a huge mantelpiece, and was continued from one end of the apartment to the other. I asked the Rajah the reason of such a structure in the apartment. He replied that he did not know, nor could any of the workmen account for it; one of them, however, took a pickaxe and dug out a portion, when, to my surprise and horror, I discovered that in this wall a human being had been bricked up. The skin was still upon the bones, which were covered with a costly dress of white muslin, spangled all over with gold; around the neck was a string of pearls; on the wrists and ankles were gold bangles, and on the feet were a pair of slippers, embroidered all over with silver wire or thread; such slippers as only Mahommedan women of rank or wealth can afford to wear. The body resembled a well-preserved mummy. The features were very distinct, and were those of a woman whose age could not at the time of her death have exceeded eighteen or nineteen years. The head was partially covered with the white dress. Long black hair was still clinging to the scalp, and was parted across the forehead and carried behind the ears. It was the most horrible and ghastly figure that I ever beheld.

The workmen appeared to take this discovery as a matter of course; or, rather, to regard it only with reference to the gold and silver ornaments upon the skeleton, and it was with great difficulty that I could prevent them stripping it, forthwith. As for the Rajah, he simply smiled and coolly remarked: 'A case of jealousy. Her husband was jealous of her, and thought her guilty, and punished her thus—bricked her up alive in this wall, with no room to move about, only standing room. Perhaps she deserved it,—perhaps she was plotting against his life; perhaps she was innocent: who can say? Hindoos as well as Mahommedans punish their wives in that way.'

'You mean that they used to do so in former times, previous to British rule in India. But such a thing could not occur in our time.'

'It does not occur so often as it did; but it does occur, sometimes, even in these days. How do you know what happens in the establishment of a wealthy native? Let us look a little further into the wall. It strikes me that we shall find some more of them.'

Orders were given accordingly to the workmen to remove with great care the whole of the ledge, in short, to pull away its entire face. This was done; and how shall I describe the awful spectacle then presented? In that wall there were no less than *five* bodies,—four besides that already alluded to. One of the number was a young man, who from his dress and the jewels on his finger-bones must have been a person of high rank; perhaps the lover of one, or both, of the young women; for he had been bricked up between two of them. The others were evidently those of confidential servants; old women, for they had grey hair. They possibly had been cognisant, or were supposed to be cognisant, of whatever offence the others had been deemed guilty.

The sun was now shining brightly on these ghastly remains, covered with garments embroidered in gold and silver. The air had a speedy effect on them, and, one by one, they fell; each forming a heap of bones, hair, shrivelled skin, dust, jewels, and finery. The latter were now gathered up, placed in a small basket, and sent to Lallah. Their value, possibly, was upwards of a thousand pounds. How many years had passed since that horrible sentence had been put into execution? Not less than one hundred and seventy, or perhaps two hundred.

Indian Society

WHILST I WAS at Agra, a distinguished military officer of high rank, who had just been appointed as a member of the Council, passed through the station on his way to the seat of government, Calcutta. It was supposed that this general officer would, on the first vacancy, become Deputy-Governor of Bengal; and of course the society of Agra was resolved to do him honour. It would not do for anybody to hang back on an occasion like this; and, for the nonce, both the civilians and the military were of one mind, and actually met on an amicable and pleasant footing, to talk the matter over, and to decide upon what was to be done. After a friendly debate, which lasted for four hours, it was resolved that Sir Gunter and Lady Gallopaway should be invited to a ball and supper, and not to a dinner. It was further determined that the entertainment should take place, not at Government-house (that would be too Civil)—not at any mess-room (that would be too Military)—but at a good-sized hall called the Metcalfe Institution, this being perfectly neutral ground. My friend, the civilian with whom I had been staying, had a perfect contempt for these local squabbles—although he was really compelled to take a part therein; and, after the meeting was over, he sat down and wrote a metrical squib, ridiculing the whole affair, and sent it for publication to one of the newspapers, the *Delhi Gazette*. For this squib—seeing that it sneered at both the civilians and the military—I unfortunately got the credit, and the consequence was, that, when I made my appearance at the ball, several of the heads of the society who had formerly received me with extreme cordiality, answered me only in monosyllables when I addressed them. Indeed, I learnt afterwards, from my friend's wife, that a meeting had actually been called to consider the propriety of not inviting me, and that I had very narrowly escaped that punishment; for had it not been for the vote of her husband my name would have been omitted, as there were ten for and ten against me, when he held up his hand in my favour.

But to the ball. There were present some twenty civilians, all dressed in black with white cravats; and each had brought with him his wife, or a sister, or daughter. Of military men (all in full dress uniform) there were about forty-five or fifty; and the ladies who came with them may have numbered thirty. In all, say that there were present—including visitors and stragglers like myself—one hundred and forty. I was rather late, and, on entering the room, beheld one of the oddest sights that I ever witnessed: all the black coats were huddled together, and so were all the reds. They had been unanimous only so far as giving the entertainment was concerned; and it seemed to be distinctly understood by each party that there was to be no mixing; and so the civilians formed quadrilles and danced with the civil ladies, and the soldiers with the military ladies. Had there been a royal regiment in Agra, there would have been three parties, owing to the jealousy that existed formerly between the Queen's and the Company's officers. Besides myself, there were two 'interlopers in the East' present at that ball. The one, a French gentleman; the other, a German Baron. They, too, were travelling about in search of the picturesque, and here they had it with a vengeance. The Frenchman could not comprehend this exclusiveness on the part of the blacks; but the German assured us that to him it was a very common sight, and to be witnessed at every ball in every garrison town in his country. 'But there,' said he, 'the military look down on the civilians, while here, it seems to me, that the civilians look down on the military. See, see! See how disdainfully that old Mrs. Revenue Board scrutinizes the dress of Mrs. Lieutenant-Colonel Damzè!'

Sure enough such was the case. 'But regard!' said the Frenchman; 'how angry is that Mrs. Sudder Adawlut, because that little Mrs. Infantry (whose husband, I am told, is the younger son of a poor English lord) is contemplating her *nez en l'air*. Truly this is a magnificent spectacle! Is it always so, I wonder?'

I was enabled, from experience, to inform him, that in almost every large station—and at Agra especially—it universally occurs; but that in small stations seldom or never.

Here we were approached by Lieutenant-Colonel Damzè himself. After exchanging a few words with the foreign gentlemen on either side of me, he passed on, seemingly proud and happy at having had an opportunity of slighting me in public, on account of the doggerel for which I had the credit.

'Mais, monsieur,' said the Frenchman to me, 'who, in wonder's name, are all these Damzè gentlemen? There is one Damzè, colonel of such a regiment; another Damzè, major in another corps. There is a Deputy Commissary-General Damzè; there is a Mr. Damzè in the Indian navy; another Damzè is a military secretary; some half dozen Damzès are, I have perceived, on the staff of the Commander-in-Chief. Parbleu! C'est Damzè—toujours Damzè! for here, by Heaven, I meet with still another Damzè! Who *are* all these Damzès?'

I informed him that Damzè was the patronymic of a nobleman in power; and with this explanation he was thoroughly enlightened, and appeared to be perfectly satisfied.

'Let us move up towards the General,' said the German Baron, who had been introduced to the old hero. 'Let us go and say a few words to him.'

It was not easy to do this; hemmed in as was the General by those who desired to make him remember them in the future. However, it was managed at last; and, somehow or other, we three interlopers contrived before long to monopolize his attention—we the only people in the room to whom he could not be of any service—for there was nothing that he could give, or get for us, if we had wanted his patronage. We, rather maliciously—so far as the crowd was concerned—stood about the distinguished old man and guarded him; and I have reason to know that he was grateful to us for so doing. Towards the hour of twelve, however, we had to stand back; for Mrs. Lieutenant-Colonel Damzè came and sat upon the sofa on the left side of the General, and talked to him in an animated but somewhat anxious manner, which became even more anxious when Mrs. Revenue Board approached, and taking a seat on the General's right (eyeing Mrs. Lieutenant-Colonel Damzè with a somewhat haughty expression), congratulated the General on his recent good fortune. At this advanced stage of the evening also, Lady Gallopaway was flanked right and left by old Mr. Revenue Board and Lieutenant-Colonel Damzè, C.B. The reader is requested to note that these two letters—C.B.—were Damzè's by right; or, at all events, that he had been recommended for the order, and that the recommendation had been instantly attended to; albeit Damzè had never been within range of an enemy's cannon in the whole course of his life. Lady Gallopaway yawned.

At length a gong sounded, and the band struck up that usual signal that supper is ready, 'O, the Roast Beef of Old England, O, the Old English Roast Beef.'

The anxiety of the ladies who sat on either side of the General was now at it height. They fanned themselves with fearful vigour; and we, the three interlopers, fancied that we could hear the palpitation of their hearts. Meanwhile their husbands, respectively, by their looks, evinced a corresponding anxiety. Each stood ready to offer his arm to Lady Gallopaway as soon as the General had made his election—of the lady he would lead to the supper table. Each party was equally confident but equally nervous, like the parties to a lawsuit. For weeks past this question of precedence had been debated in Agra, and very warmly debated—namely, whether Mrs. Revenue Board, of the Civil Service, or Mrs. Lieutenant-Colonel Damzè, C.B., was entitled to the *pas*. Now was the moment for a decision, or at all events an authority in support of either position or argument. The old General (upon whom both Mr. Revenue Board and Lieutenant-Colonel Damzè, C.B., had their anxious eyes) rose, smiled, bowed to the ladies who had flanked him, left them, and wandered about the ball-room, looking to the right and left, as if searching for some one. Presently he stopped short before little Mrs. Infantry, who was talking to a cornet of the 17th Light Cavalry. The General offered her his arm. She took it very graciously, and was led away. But before leaving the room she halted, turned round, and stared very significantly at the two elderly ladies who were still seated on the sofa, overwhelmed in surprise, horror, and indignation. Infantry, who was only a lieutenant in his regiment, observing that the General had recognised the social right of his wife, which she had derived solely from him, instantly rushed up to Lady Gallopaway, and offered her an arm (which she took), led her away in triumph, leaving his own Colonel (Damzè) and old Mr. Revenue Board gasping and gaping at each other in mutual disgust and consternation. Had a shell burst in the building, had the powder magazine exploded and shattered all the windows, the commotion could scarcely have been greater than it was at that moment. No one could account for this extraordinary conduct, or caprice, as it was termed, on the part of the old General. Damzè, who had just been flattering him concerning his wonderful achievements, now declared that 'the old fool had become half-witted since eighteen hundred and forty-seven,' while Revenue Board, who a quarter of an hour previously had, to the General's face, held forth on the unflinching independence which had marked his character through life, now protested—openly protested—that he had been a time-server throughout his entire career, and had some object in thus truckling before the son of an influential peer! The ladies on the sofa stared at each other; now commiseratingly and in silence for at least two minutes, then simultaneously ejaculated: 'What *can* it mean!'

'I thought it would have been me,' said Mrs. Revenue Board.

'You?' said Mrs. Damzè.

'Yes; why not? My husband is a civilian of twenty years' standing.'

'Is not my husband a Lieutenant-Colonel and a C.B.? If he were only a Major and a C.B. he would take precedence of Mr. Revenue Board.'

'You are quite mistaken.'

'Indeed not. Do you suppose a C.B. goes for nothing?'

'No; but——'

Here Lieutenant-Colonel Damzè and Mr. Revenue Board, who had been discussing the same question, but in a calmer spirit than their wives, approached, and, making common cause against the upstart enemy (Infantry and his wife), formed a quartette and went into the supper room; where, to their intense mortification, they heard little Mrs. Infantry talking loudly, on purpose to attract the notice of all present. What was even more mortifying still, the old General was paying her marked attention.

The red party, that is to say, the military, were in very high spirits; the black, the civilians, correspondingly depressed.

The quartette, consisting of Damzè and Revenue Board, and their wives, ate voraciously, but evidently without appetite. They sipped their wine with an absent formality, which was very entertaining to lookers-on, who were in no way interested in the momentous question which was preying on their very souls.

'It shall not end here,' said Damzè, moodily fixing his eyes on the chandelier.

'Not, indeed!' said Mr. Revenue Board.

'I shall put my case to the Governor-General direct,' said Damzè. 'His Lordship is a near connexion of mine.'

'I am perfectly aware of that,' said Mr. Revenue Board; 'but it is my intention to submit my case to his Lordship through Mr. Bommerson, the Lieutenant-Governor of these provinces, officially; and, if his Lordship's opinion should be adverse, I shall have my appeal to the Court of Directors, amongst whom, thank Heaven! I have several relations and warm friends.'

'And you will write, I hope, my dear,' said Mrs. Revenue Board, 'to Sir John Bobgrouse, who is the President of the Board of Control, and whose secretary married your first cousin—recollect!'

'*We* can write, too,' said Mrs. Lieutenant-Colonel Damzè.

'You may write to anybody you please,' said Mrs. Revenue Board, defiantly and contemptuously; 'but you will remember that the point between us is this—that even if your husband, in consequence of having got, no matter how, a C.B.ship, has the right to precede my husband, a civilian of twenty years' standing—whether you have the right to precede me? That is the question; and I hope, Revenue dear, you will not fail to raise it.'

Reader, the question was submitted in all its bearings for the consideration of the Most Noble the Governor-General of India, who, declining to take upon himself so fearful a responsibility, referred the matter to the Home Government. Leadenhall-street had something to say to it, and so had the Board of Control. While the case was pending, the newspapers in every part of India literally teemed with letters on the subject, and their editors were invited to give their opinions thereon. Only one of the number was weak enough to do this, and bitterly did he repent of his rashness; for, having decided in favour of the C.B. and of Mrs. C.B., he lost (so he confessed to me) no less than six-and-twenty civilians (each of twenty years' standing) in his subscription-list. For more than eighteen months this precedence question formed a leading topic, not only in the public prints, but in private circles. It became, in short, a perfect nuisance. At length the decision of the Home Government came out to India; but, alas! they had only half done their work. They had given C.B. the precedence over the civilian of twenty years' standing, but had been silent about their wives! So, the matter was 'referred back.' A clerk in the Private Secretary's office told me that he was occupied for three hours in copying only the Governor-General's minute on the Court's despatch, which was a very lengthy one, and signed by the chairman for himself and the other directors, whose names were given in full. He further informed me that the whole of the documents connected with this weighty affair would, if put into type, form a volume five times as bulky as Sir William Napier's *Conquest of Scinde*!

How the matter was settled eventually I do not know; for, when I left India, the question had not been decided. On the great point, when it was referred for a second time to the Home Authorities, there was a difference of opinion between the Court of Directors and the Board of Control, and a long correspondence ensued on the subject, between each of these departments of the Indian Government and the Governor-General, who was required to have the case laid before the Advocates-General of the Supreme Courts at the various Presidencies. These gentlemen differed one with the other in their views of the case, each alleging that the point lay in a nutshell, and was as clear as possible. For all I know to the contrary, it may be in the nutshell at this moment. Both Lieutenant-Colonel Damzè and Mr. Revenue Board laid 'cases' before the Calcutta barristers, who pocketed their fees, and laconically expressed their opinions respectively, that the parties who consulted them were in the right— 'there could be no doubt on the point,' they said. Damzè sent a copy of his case, and the opinion of his barrister thereon, to Revenue Board, who rather triumphantly returned the compliment. I regret to say, that this contest engendered in Agra a great deal of what is called bad blood, and induced many ladies to descend to very unseemly personalities. For instance, Mrs. Damzè one evening, at the band-stand, told Mrs. Revenue Board, that when she (Mrs. R. B.) returned to England, she would have no rank at all, as her husband was not an esquire even—but a 'mister' in his own country. To which Mrs. Revenue Board replied:—

'And you, pray? Is not your husband in the Company's service?'

'Yes,' rejoined Mrs. Damzè; 'but you forget the C.B.!'

Let us now return to the Honourable Lieutenant Infantry. When that officer came up, and led away Lady Gallopaway to supper, Damzè was overheard to say, 'I'll take the shine out of that young gentleman.' And, if taking the shine meant constantly bullying the subaltern, Damzè certainly kept his word. And when the next hot weather came, and the Lieutenant wished to accompany his sick wife to the Hills, Damzè, when he forwarded the application for six months' leave of absence, wrote privately to the Assistant Adjutant-General, and recommended that it should not be granted. The honourable subaltern, however, was rather too strong for his colonel, in the way of interest. Presuming on the acquaintance which existed between his father and the Commander-in-Chief, he wrote a letter to that functionary, and a few days afterwards found himself in general orders. The wrath of Damzè may be easily imagined, especially as he had boasted to several of his officers of having put a spoke in the Lieutenant's wheel. And by way of throwing salt upon the Colonel's wounds, the Lieutenant called upon him, and, in the politest manner possible, inquired if there was anything he could do for him at head-quarters.

~

While at Agra, a Bengalee Baboo called upon me. Judging from his appearance, I should have guessed his age to be about fifty years; but he was upwards of seventy. He spoke English with marvellous fluency and accuracy, and could read and write the language as well and as elegantly as any educated European. He was, perhaps, the cleverest Hindoo whom I encountered during my sojourn in the East. His manners were peculiarly courteous and winning, and there was an air of penitence about the man, which, apart from his abilities, induced me to treat him with kindness and consideration. His name was—let us say—Nobinkissen.

The history of Nobinkissen was simply this. He was a Brahmin of the highest caste, and, at the age of eighteen, was a writer in the service of the government, on a salary of ten rupees per month. He ingratiated himself with every civilian under whom he served, and gradually rose, step by step, until he became the Sheristadar, or head clerk, of a circuit-judge of a court of appeal. In this office he acquired riches, and was still adding to his store, when his official career was brought prematurely to a close.

I must here inform the reader that not one civilian in a hundred, no matter what his rank or grade, can read and write Hindostanee or Persian, although the majority of them have some colloquial knowledge of both those languages. Yet, as a matter of course, they append their signatures to every document of which, on hearing it read aloud to them by their native officials, they approve. Their orders they dictate orally; those orders are transcribed by the Sheristadar, who gives them to a native writer to copy. This done, they are read aloud for correction or approval, and then signed in English by the covenanted civilian. Before leaving office every day, such civilian may have to sign fifty, sixty, or a hundred documents; for the rule is, not to sign each of them when read, but to sign them in a mass at the breaking-up of the court. Here Nobinkissen invented his means of money making. Whenever the judge gave a decree in any case of importance, he made a counterpart of such decree, and when the signing time came, obtained, without any sort of trouble or inquiry, the signature of the Sahib and the seal of the Court to both documents. He was thus, to all intents and purposes—or, at all events, for his own—in possession of something tantamount to the fee-simple of the lands in dispute. He could arm either the appellant or the respondent with the final decree of the Court, under the hand and official seal of the judge. The only question with him now was, which of the litigants would give the most money, and to each, in private, and in the Sahib's name, he exhibited the documents. The highest bidder, of course, gained the day, whereupon Nobinkissen took the coin, handed over one of the decrees, and burnt the other.

It fell out that Nobinkissen was attacked with fever, and, in a state bordering on delirium, he parted with, that is to say, sold, to both respondent and appellant, a decree, under the hand and seal of the judge, such decree arming the holder with the power to take possession of a very large estate in Bengal. Each party, fearful of a disturbance, which often occurs when possession of an estate is sought for, applied to the magistrate of a district, under a certain regulation of government, for assistance, in order to enable him to carry out the judge's decree, which each, as a matter of course, produced. The magistrate was naturally much perplexed, and made a reference to the judge, who could only say he had signed but one decree. There was then a report made to the government by the magistrate. An investigation ensued, and the judge was, meanwhile, suspended, for great suspicion lurked in the minds of many that he was not so innocent as he affected to be. When Nobinkissen recovered from his sickness, and saw the dilemma in which his superior, the judge, was placed, he made a clean breast of it, and confessed that the guilt was his, and his alone. Nobinkissen was tried, convicted, and sentenced to be imprisoned in irons for the term of his natural life. For nine years he was in the gaol at Alipore, near Calcutta. At the expiration of that period he was called upon to furnish some information of which he was possessed, in relation to certain public affairs. He was brought from the prison, confronted with several officials, amongst whom was a member of the council. His altered appearance, his emaciated form, his attitude of despair, and the intelligence and readiness with which he responded to the questions put to him, touched the hearts of those by whom he was examined, and the member of council, who has been since a director of the East India Company, spoke to the Governor-General, and eventually obtained Nobinkissen's pardon and release. The Hindoos and Mussulmans in India (like the Arabs) do not regard being guilty of a fraud or theft as a disgrace. The degrading part of the business is, being convicted, and Nobinkissen, on being set at liberty, could not face his countrymen in Bengal, and therefore retired to the Upper Provinces, where he lived in comparative obscurity, and in easy circumstances, for he had not disgorged his ill-gotten gains. His wife had taken care of them during his captivity.

At the time that Nobinkissen called upon me, the

government of India were in considerable difficulty in respect to finance. A new loan had been opened, but it did not fill, and the government had very wisely determined upon closing it. Nobinkissen made this a topic of conversation, and his views—albeit they came from a man who had been convicted of a fraud—are, at the present time especially, entitled to the very gravest consideration.

'Ah, sir!' he remarked, 'it is a pitiful thing that the government of a great empire like this should ever be in pecuniary difficulties and put to their wits' end for a few millions annually, in order to make the receipts square with the expenditure.'

'But how can it be helped?' I asked.

'Easily, sir,' he replied. 'Why not make it expedient to do away with the perpetual settlement of Lord Cornwallis, and resettle the whole of Bengal? That is by far the most fertile province in the East; but it is taxed lighter than even these poor lands of the Upper Provinces. Look at the Durbungah Rajah. Nearly the whole of Tirhoot, the garden of India, belongs to him, and he does not pay into the government treasury half a lac (five thousand pounds) per annum, while his collections amount to upwards of twenty lacs. These are the men who get hold of the money and bury it, and keep it from circulating.'

'But all zemindarees (lands) are not so profitable in Bengal?'

'No; many are not worth holding—especially the smaller ones, although the land is just as good, and just as well cultivated.'

'But how is that?'

'They are so heavily taxed. You must know, sir, that in those days—the days of Lord Cornwallis—the greatest frauds were committed, in respect to the perpetual settlement. The natives who were about, and under, the settlement officers all made immense fortunes, and the zemindars from whom they took their bribes have profited ever since to the cost of the poorer zemindars, who could not or would not bribe, and to the cost of the British government. It is a great mistake to suppose that the whole of the landholders in Bengal would cry out against a resettlement of that province. Only men holding vast tracts of country, at a comparatively nominal rent, would cry out.'

'And tax the British government with a breach of faith?'

'Yes. But what need the government care for that cry, especially when its act is not only expedient, but would be just withal? In Bengal, all the great zemindars are rich, very rich men. In these provinces, with very, very few exceptions, they are poor, so that the whole of Upper India would be glad to see the perpetual settlement done away with, and the land resettled.'

'Why so?'

'That is only human—and, certainly, Asiatic—nature. Few of us like to behold our neighbours better off than ourselves; so that the cry of faith-breaking would not meet with a response in this part of the world.'

'Yes; but in Europe the cry would be too powerful to contend against. The Exeter Hall orators and the spouters at the Court of Proprietors would—'

'Ah, sir! India should either be governed in India or in England. It is the number of wheels in the government that clogs the movement of the machine.'

'Very true.'

'But who are these men—these zemindars with whom you are required to keep an implicit faith? Are they your friends? If so, why do they never come forward to assist you in your difficulties? Did a single zemindar, when, after the battle of Ferozeshah, the empire was shaking in the balance, lift a finger to help the government of India? And, tomorrow, if your rule were at stake, and dependent on their assistance, think you they would render it? Think you they would furnish money if your treasury was exhausted? Not one pice! Think you they would furnish men to protect your stations denuded of troops? No! Although hundreds of them can each turn out a thousand or two of followers, armed with iron-bound bludgeons, swords, and shields, when they desire to intimidate an European indigo-planter, or to fight a battle between themselves about a boundary question. These are the men who, in your greatest need, would remain neutral until, if it so happened, you were brought to your last gasp, when, as one man, they would not fail to rise and give you the final blow.'

'Do you believe that? I do not.'

'Sir, I know my own countrymen better than you do.'

'If such a state of affairs were to come about, and these zemindars remained neutral, of course the cry of breaking faith would be absurd in the extreme. Neutrality, in such a case, would be almost as bad as hostility.'

[Nobinkissen's prophecy has been fulfilled to the letter. Our rule has been at stake, in imminent peril, and not one of these men has offered to assist us with men or money. The Rajahs of Durbungah and Burdwan alone, to say nothing of the Newab of Moorshedabad, between them could have furnished an army of, at the very least, five thousand stalwart fighting men, whereas they have looked upon our difficulties in perfect apathy. It is from the coffers of men of this stamp that large sums should be extracted annually towards keeping up a vast—an overwhelming—European force in India. Faith with such men as these! What claim have they to our faintest consideration! What right to expect that we shall any longer forego the collection of several extra millions annually—several extra millions which, to every intent and purpose, is our just due?]

'There is a line in Shakespeare, sir,' Nobinkissen continued, 'which the government of India should adopt as its motto, and act up to consistently—

'Cæsar never does wrong without just cause.'

Our conversation was here interrupted by a noise in the road. I went to the window, and observing a great crowd, inquired of one of my servants who was standing in the verandah:—

'What is the matter?'

'A bullock has fallen down, and they are trying to get him up—that is all, Sahib,' was the reply.

I rushed to the spot, followed by Nobinkissen, and there beheld a scene which in no other country would have been tolerated by the crowd assembled.

One of a pair of bullocks, drawing an over-laden cart, had from weakness and fatigue, sank beneath the burden. The driver of the animals (a Hindoo) had broken, by twisting it violently, the tail of the poor beast, which was nothing but skin and bone, and was covered with wounds from ill-treatment. Heavy blows and the tail breaking having failed to make the jaded ox stand upon his legs, the driver—heedless of my remonstrance—collected some straw and sticks and lighted a fire all round him. The poor beast now struggled very hard, but was unable to rise, and presently he resigned himself to be scorched to death.

'I always thought that the cow was a sacred animal with Hindoos?' said I to Nobinkissen.

'Yes,' said he.

'And here is a Hindoo who works one of his gods till he drops down with sheer fatigue, and then cruelly puts him to death!'

'Yes, that often happens,' said Nobinkissen, smiling.

'Then, what an absurdity and inconsistency for the Hindoos at Benares, and other holy places, to make such a noise if an European only strikes a sacred animal with a whip! Why, it was only the other day that a mob collected around the house of the magistrate and set the authorities at defiance: all because the magistrate had ordered that one of the bulls which crowd the streets should be shut up, on the ground that he had gored several people.'

'That is the doing of the Brahmins, who incite the people to such acts; and every concession on the part of the government leads those Brahmins to believe that they have great power, and leads the people also to believe it. If a Mahommedan finds one of those bulls in the way, and gives him a thrashing with a thick stick, or probes him in the side with a sword, the Brahmins say nothing, nor do the people of Benares.'

'Why is that?'

'Because it would not be worth while. The strife would be profitless; for, you see, sir, the Mahommedans are not the rulers of this country, but the Sahibs are; and hence the jealousy with which they are watched. In time, the Government of India will see the necessity of forbidding Hindoo festivals in the public streets—abolishing them—just as Suttee was abolished. It is only the dissolute rich and the rabble who take any delight in these festivals, many of which are indecent and disgusting. Sensible and respectable Hindoos take no part in them; on the contrary, they avoid them, and think them a nuisance. Hindooism will never become extinct, so long as this world lasts; but the British Government has the power of doing away with those obnoxious observances in the public thoroughfares, which only disfigure the religion.'

'Well, in that case, you would have to do away with the Mahommedan festivals?'

'Most certainly—in the public streets. In private, the Mahommedans as well as the Hindoos might be permitted to keep their festivals in whatever way they thought proper. Do you suppose that the Mahommedans, when in power, suffered the Hindoos to block up the streets continually with their processions, as they do now? Think you that they entertained the same consideration for the bulls and the monkeys at Benares as the British now entertain?

And when, in turn, the Mahrattas overran this part of the country, think you that Agra was ever deafened, as it now is, with the din of the Buckree Ede and the Mohurrum?'

'Perhaps not. But then you see, Nobinkissen, we are a tolerant people, and wish to convince both creeds that we have no desire to interfere with their religious prejudices in any way whatsoever.'

'Yes; but then you are inconsistent, and the consequence is, that you not only get the credit of being insincere, but are imposed upon to the utmost.'

'How, inconsistent!'

'Why, you declare that you have no desire to interfere with the religious prejudices of the Hindoo and the Mahommedan; but you, nevertheless, encourage missionary gentlemen to go from station to station to preach in the open air concerning the superiority of your religion over all others. Believe me, sir, this does a great deal of harm.'

'Ah! but we make converts!'

'How many do you suppose?'

'I cannot say.'

'I can. Take India from one end to the other, and you make, annually, one out of fifty thousand.'

'No more?'

'No more, sir! That is the result of preaching in the open air, all over the country, and the distribution of thousands and hundreds of thousands of tracts printed in the Hindostanee and Bengalee languages.

'Well, that is something, Nobinkissen.'
'And of what class of people are your converts?'
'Respectable men of all classes, I suppose.'
'The dregs of both Hindoos and Mussulmans. The most debased and degraded of Indians—men who only assume Christianity in the hope of temporal advantage and preferment—and who fling aside their newly put-on faith, and laugh and scoff at your credulity the moment they find their hope frustrated. I could give you at least one hundred instances; but one will suffice. Not long ago a Mussulman, named Ally Khan, was converted by Mr. Jones, a missionary in Calcutta, and, shortly after his conversion, obtained an appointment with a salary of one hundred rupees a month, in the Baptist Missionary Society. Here he contrived to embezzle sixteen hundred rupees, for which offence he was indicted in the Supreme Court, found guilty, and sentenced to a year's imprisonment in the Calcutta gaol. On hearing the sentence he exclaimed: 'In the name of the devil, is this the reward of renouncing my religion? Farewell, Christianity! From this hour I am a Moslem again!'

'Another very flagrant case occurred in this very station. A civilian took into his service a recently converted Hindoo, as a sirdar-bearer. The fellow had charge of a money-bag, and ran off with it. And where and how do you suppose he was apprehended? At Hurdwar, taking an active part in the Hoolee Festival! The Roman Catholic priests have long since left off asking the natives of India to become Christians. Those who voluntarily present themselves, are, after a strict examination, and a due warning that they must hope for no temporal advantage, admitted into the Church.'

'And do they have any applications?'

'Very very few, indeed; but those whom they admit do, really and truly, become Christians.'

These last words of Nobinkissen were scarcely pronounced, when a palkee was brought up to my door, and out of it stepped a Roman Catholic priest—an Italian gentleman, a Jesuit—whom I had met a few evenings previously at the house of a mutual friend. Nobinkissen, who appeared to know the reverend father intimately, related to him the substance of the conversation we had just held, or rather the latter part thereof, and the priest corroborated every allegation that Nobinkissen had made.

'Yea,' he added, 'we now devote our attention, exclusively, to the spiritual wants of the white man who requires our aid—convinced, as we are, of the hopelessness of the task of converting the Hindoo and the Mussulman to Christianity.' And, in addition to the instances of false converts afforded by Nobinkissen, he did not scruple to detail several others of an equally atrocious character and complexion.

Churchyards, etc

I CANNOT LEAVE Meerut without taking the reader to the churchyard of that station.

An Indian churchyard presents a very different aspect to a churchyard in England or elsewhere. The tombs for the most part are very much larger. When first erected or newly done up they are as white as snow, formed, as they are generally, of chunam (plaster), which somewhat resembles Roman cement; but after exposure to only one rainy season and one hot weather, they become begrimed and almost black. The birds flying from structure to structure carry with them the seeds of various plants and herbs, and these if not speedily removed take root and grow apace. A stranger wandering in the churchyard of Meerut might fancy that he is amidst ruins of stupendous antiquity, if he were not aware of the fact that fifty years have scarcely elapsed since the first Christian corpse was deposited within those walls which now encircle some five acres of ground, literally covered with tombs, in every stage of preservation and decay. I was conducted in my ramble through the Meerut churchyard by an old and very intelligent pensioner, who had originally been a private in a regiment of Light Dragoons.

This old man lived by the churchyard, that is to say, he derived a very comfortable income from looking after and keeping in repair the tombs of those whose friends are now far away; but whose thoughts nevertheless still turn occasionally to that Christian enclosure in the land of heathens and idolaters.

'I get, sir, for this business,' said the old man, pointing with his stick to a very magnificent edifice, 'two pounds a year. It is not much, but it is what I asked, and it pays me very well, sir. And if you should go back to England, and ever come across any of her family, I hope, sir, you will tell them that I do my duty by the grave; not that I think they have any doubt of it, for they must know—or, leastways, they have been told by them they can believe—that if I never received a farthing from them I would always keep it in repair, as it is now. God bless her, and rest her soul! She was as good and as beautiful a woman as ever trod this earth.'

'Who was she?'

'The wife of an officer in my old regiment, sir. I was in her husband's troop. He's been out twice since the regiment went home, only to visit this grave; for he has long since sold out of the service, and is a rich gentleman. The last time he came was about five years ago. He comes what you call *incog.*; nobody knows who he is, and he never calls on anybody. All that he now does in this country is to come here, stop for three days and nights, putting up at the dâk bungalow, and spending his time here, crying. It is there that he stands, where you stand now, fixing his eyes on the tablet, and sometimes laying his head down on the stone, and calling out her name: 'Ellen! Ellen! My own dear Ellen!' He did love her, surely, sir.'

'Judging from the age of the lady, twenty-three, and the date of her death, he must be rather an old man now.'

'Yes, sir. He must be more than sixty; but his love for her memory is just as strong as ever. She died of a fever, poor thing. And for that business,' he again pointed with his stick to a tomb admirably preserved, 'I used to get two pounds ten shillings a year. That is the tomb of a little girl of five years old, the daughter of a civilian. The parents are now dead. They must be, for I have not heard of 'em or received anything from 'em for more than six years past.'

'Then who keeps the tomb in repair?'

'I do, sir. When I am here, with my trowel and mortar, and whitewash, why shouldn't I make the outside of the little lady's last home on earth as bright and as fair as those of her friends and neighbours? I have a nursery of 'em, as I call it, over in yonder corner—the children's corner. Some of 'em are paid for, others not; but when I'm there doing what's needful, I touch 'em up all alike, bless their dear little souls. And somehow or other every good action meets its own reward, and often when we least expect it. Now, for instance, sir, about three years and a half ago, I was over there putting the nursery in good order, when up comes a grey-headed gentleman, and looks about the graves. Suddenly he stopped opposite to one and began to read, and presently he took out his pocket handkerchief and put it to his eyes.

'Did you know that little child, sir?' said I, when it was not improper to speak. 'Know it?' said he, 'yes. It was my own little boy.' 'Dear me, sir!' I answered him. 'And you are, then, Lieutenant Statterleigh?' 'I was,' said he; 'but I am now the colonel of a regiment that has just come to India, and is now stationed at Dinapore. But tell me, who keeps this grave in order?' 'I do, sir,' says I. 'At whose expense?' says he. 'At nobody's, sir,' says I. 'It is kept in order by the dictates of my own conscience. Your little boy is in good company here; and while I am whitening the tombs of the other little dears, I have it not in my heart to pass by his without giving it a touch also.' Blest if he didn't take me to the house where he was staying, and give me five hundred rupees! That sort of thing has happened to me more than five or six times in my life, not that I ever hope or think of being paid for such work and labour when I am about it.'

'That must have been a magnificent affair,' said I, pointing to a heap of red stone and marble. 'But how comes it in ruins?'

'It is just as it was left, sir. The lady died. Her husband, a judge here, took on terribly; and ordered that tomb for her. Some of the stone was brought from Agra, some from Delhi; but before it was put together and properly erected, he married again, and the work was stopped. I was present at the funeral. There was no getting him away after the service was over, and at last they had to resort to force and violence—in fact, to carry him out of the yard. But the shallowest waters, as the proverb says, sir, always make the most noise, while those are the deepest that flow on silently. Yonder is a funny tomb, sir,' continued the old man, again pointing with his stick. 'There! close to the tomb of the lady which I first showed you.'

'How do you mean funny?' I asked, observing nothing particular in the structure.

'Well, sir, it is funny only on account of the history of the two gentlemen whose remains it covers,' replied the old man, leading me to the tomb. 'One of these young gentlemen, sir, was an officer—a lieutenant—in the Bengal Horse Artillery; the other was an ensign in a Royal Regiment of the Line. There was a ball, and by some accident that beautiful lady of our regiment had engaged herself to both of them for the same dance. When the time came, both went up and claimed her hand. Neither of them would give way, and the lady not wishing to offend either by showing a preference, and finding herself in a dilemma, declined to dance with either. Not satisfied with this, they retired to the verandah, where they had some high words, and the next morning they met, behind the church there, and fought a duel, in which both of them fell, mortally wounded. They had scarcely time to shake hands with one another when they died. In those days matters of the kind were very easily hushed up; and it was given out, though everybody knew to the contrary, that one had died of fever and the other of cholera, and they were both buried side by side in one grave; and this tomb was erected over them at the joint expense of the two regiments to which they belonged. I get ten rupees a year for keeping this grave in order.'

'Who pays you?'

'A gentleman in Calcutta, a relation of one of them. I'll tell you what it is, sir. This foolish affair, which ended so fatally, sowed the seeds of the fever that carried off that beautiful and good woman yonder. She was maddened by the thought of being the cause of the quarrel in which they lost their lives. I knew them both, sir, from seeing them so often on the parade ground and at the band-stand; very fine young men they were, sir. Yes; here they sleep in peace.'

'Whose tombs are those?' I asked, pointing to some two or three hundred which were all exactly alike, and in three straight lines; in other words, three deep.

'Those are the tombs of the men of the Cameronians, sir. These graves are all uniform, as you observe. Fever made sad havoc with that regiment. They lost some three companies in all. Behind them are the tombs of the men of the Buffs, and behind them the tombs of the men of other Royal Regiments of Infantry—all uniform you see, sir; but those of each regiment rather differently shaped. To the right, flanking the Infantry tombs, are the tombs of the men of the Cavalry, 8th and 11th Dragoons, and 16th Lancers. In the rear of the Cavalry are the tombs of the Horse and Foot Artillerymen—all uniform you see, sir. Egad! if they could rise just now, what a pretty little army they would form, of all ranks, some thousands of 'em, and well officered, too, they would be; and here a man to lead them. This is the tomb of Major-General Considine, one of the most distinguished men in the British army. He was the officer that the Duke of Wellington fixed upon to bring the 53rd Foot into good order, when they ran riot in Gibraltar some years ago. This is the tomb of General Considine, rotting and going rapidly to decay, though it was only built in the year 1845. A great deal of money is squandered in the churchyards in India. Tombs are erected, and at a great expense frequently. After they are once put up it is very seldom that they are visited or heeded. Tens of thousands of pounds have been thrown away on the vast pile of bricks and mortar and stone that you now see within this enclosure, and with the exception of a few all are crumbling away. A Hindoo—a sweeper—said to me the other day in this graveyard, 'Why don't you English burn your dead as we do, instead of leaving their graves here, to tell us how much you can neglect them and how little you care for them? What is the use of whitening a few sepulchres amidst this mass of black ruin?' I had no answer to give the fellow, sir; indeed the same thought had often occurred to me while at work in this wilderness. Do you not think, sir, that the government, through its own executive officers, ought to expend a few hundred pounds every year on these yards, in order to avert such a scandal and disgrace? I do not speak interestedly. I have as much already on my hands as I can perform, if not more; but I do often think that there is really some reason in the remarks of that sweeper. All these graves that you see here so blackened and left to go to ruin, are the graves of men who have served their country and died in its service. Very little money would keep the yard free from this grass and these rank weeds, and very little more would make all these tombs fit to be seen; for neither labour nor whitewash is expensive in this part of the world. One would hardly suppose, on looking about him just now, that the sons and daughters of some of the best families in England are buried here, and that in a very short time no one will be able to distinguish the spot where each is lying; so defaced and so much alike will all the ruins become. What, sir, I repeat, is the use of throwing away money in building tombs, if they are not kept in repair? Instead of laying out fifty or a hundred pounds on a thing like this, why not lay out only five pounds on a single head-stone, and put the rest out at interest to keep it up?'

'Or a small slab with an iron railing round it?'

'Ah, sir; but then you would require an European to remain here, and a couple of native watchmen to see that the railings were not carried off by the villagers. As it is, they never allow an iron railing to remain longer than a week, or so long as that. They watch for an opportunity, jump over this low wall, and tear them down, or wrench them off and away with them.'

'But surely there is some one to watch the yard?'

'Yes, two sweepers—men of the lowest caste of Hindoos. And when it is found out that a grave has been plundered of its railings, or that the little marble tablet, which some have, has been taken away, they deny all knowledge of the matter, and are simply discharged, and two others of the same caste are put into their places. It would not be much to build a comfortable little bungalow for an European—a man like myself, for instance—and give the yard into his charge, holding him responsible for any damage done, and requiring him to see that the grave of every Christian—man, woman, and child—is kept in good order. But horrible as is the condition of this churchyard—looking as it does, for the most part, more like a receptacle for the bodies of felons than those of good and brave soldiers and civilians, and their wives and children—it is really nothing when compared with the graveyard of Kernaul. Kernaul, you know, sir, was our great frontier station some twenty years ago. It was, in fact, as large a station as Umballah now is. It had its church, its playhouse, its barracks for cavalry, infantry, and artillery, its mess-houses, magnificent bungalows, and all the rest of it. For some reason or other—but what that reason was I could, never discover, nor anybody else to my knowledge—the station was abandoned with all its buildings, which cost the government and private individuals lacs and lacs of rupees. You may be pretty sure that the villagers were not long in plundering every house that was unprotected. Away went the doors and windows, the venetians, and every bar, bolt, nail, or bit of iron upon which they could lay their fingers; not content with this, the brutes set fire to many or nearly all of the thatched bungalows, in the hope of picking up something amongst the ruins. The church—the largest and best in the Upper Provinces, with no one to take care of it— was one of the first places that suffered. Like the other buildings, it was despoiled of its doors, windows, benches, bolts, nails, &c., and they carried away every marble tablet therein erected, and removeable without much difficulty. And the same kind of havoc was made in the burial-ground— the tombs were smashed, some of the graves, and especially the vaults, opened; and plainly enough was it to be seen, that the low caste men had broken open the coffins and examined their contents, in the hope of finding a ring, or an ear-ring, or some other ornament on the person of the dead. I went there a year ago on some business connected with the grave of a lady, whose husband wished her remains to be removed to Meerut, and placed in the same vault with those of his sister, who died here about eighteen months since. I was not successful, however. There was no trace of her tomb. It was of stone, and had been taken away bodily, to pave the elephant shed or camel yard, perhaps, of some rich native in the neighbourhood. Looking around me, as I did, and remembering Kernaul when it was crowded with Europeans, it seemed to me as though the British had been turned out of the country by the natives, and that the most sacred spot in the cantonment had been desecrated out of spite or revenge. And it is just what they would do if ever they got the upper hand.'

[Whilst I write, it has just occurred to me that this old soldier and his family perished in the massacre at Meerut on the 10th of May. He was in some way related to, or connected by marriage with, Mrs. Courtenay, the keeper of the hotel, who, with her nieces, was so barbarously murdered on that disastrous occasion.]

'Why, bless my soul!' exclaimed the old man, stooping down and picking up something, 'if the old gentleman hasn't shed his skin again! This is the skin of a very large snake, a cobra capella, that I have known for the last thirteen years. He must be precious old from his size, the slowness of his movements, and the bad cough he has had for the last four or five years. Last winter he was very bad indeed, and I thought he was going to die. He was then living in the ruins of old General Webster's vault and coughing continually, just like a man with the asthma. However, I strewed a lot of fine ashes and some bits of wool in the ruin to keep him warm by night, and some fine white sand at the entrance, upon which he used to crawl out and bask, when the sun had made it hot enough; and when the warm weather set in he got all right again.'

'Rather a strange fancy of yours, to live upon such amicable terms with the great enemy of the human race?'

'Well, perhaps it is. But he once bit and killed a thief who came here to rob a child's grave of the iron railings, which its parents, contrary to my advice, had placed round it, and ever since then I have liked the snake, and have never thought of molesting him. I have had many an opportunity of killing him (if I had wished to do it) when I have caught him asleep on the tombstones, in the winter's sun. I could kill him this very day—this very hour—if I liked, for I know where he is at this very moment. He is in a hole, close to the Ochterlony monument there, in that corner of the yard. But why should I hurt him? He has never offered to do me any harm, and when I sing, as I sometimes do, when I am alone here at work on some tomb or other, he will crawl up, and listen for two or three hours together. One morning, while he was listening, he came in for a good meal which lasted him some days.'

'How was this?'

'I will tell you, sir. A minar was chased by a small hawk, and in despair came and perched itself on the top of a most lofty tomb at which I was at work. The hawk, with his eyes fixed intently on his prey, did not, I fancy, see the snake lying motionless in the grass; or if he did see him he did not think he was a snake, but something else—my crowbar, perhaps. After a little while the hawk pounced down, and was just about to give the minar a blow and a grip, when the snake suddenly lifted his head, raised his hood, and hissed. The hawk gave a shriek, fluttered, flapped his wings with all his might, and tried very hard to fly away. But it would not do. Strong as the eye of the hawk was, the eye of the snake was stronger. The hawk for a time seemed suspended in the air; but at last he was obliged to come down, and sit opposite to the old gentleman (the snake) who commenced, with his forked tongue, and keeping his eyes upon him all the while, to slime his victim all over. This occupied him for at least forty minutes, and by the time the process was over the hawk was perfectly motionless. I don't think he was dead. But he was very soon, however, for the old gentleman put him into a coil or two, and crackled up every bone in the hawk's body. He then gave him another sliming, made a big mouth, distended his neck till it was as big round as the thickest part of my arm, and down went the hawk like a shin of beef into a beggarman's bag.'

'And what became of the minar?'

'He was off like a shot, sir, the moment his enemy was in trouble, and no blame to him. What a funny thing nature is altogether, sir! I very often think of that scene when I am at work here.'

'But this place must be infested with snakes?'

'I have never seen but that one, sir, and I have been here for a long time. Would you like to see the old gentleman, sir? As the sun is up, and the morning rather warm, perhaps he will come out, if I pretend to be at work and give him a ditty. If he does not, we will look in upon him.'

'Come along,' said I.

I accompanied the old man to a tomb, close to the monument beneath which the snake was said to have taken up his abode. I did not go very near to the spot, but stood upon a tomb with a thick stick in my hand, quite prepared to slay the monster if he approached me; for from childhood I have always had an instinctive horror of reptiles of every species, caste, and character.

The old man began to hammer away with his mallet and chisel, and to sing a very quaint old song which I had never heard before, and have never heard since. It was a dialogue or duet between the little finger and the thumb, and began thus. The thumb said:

'Dear Rose Mary Green!
When I am king, little finger, you shall be queen.'

The little finger replied:

'Who told you so, Thummy, Thummy? Who told you so?'

The thumb responded:

'It was my own heart, little finger, who told me so!'

The thumb then drew a very flattering picture of the life they would lead when united in wedlock, and concluded, as nearly as I can remember, thus:

Thumb.

'And when you are dead, little finger, as it may hap,
You shall be buried, little finger, under the tap.'

Little Finger.

'Why, Thummy, Thummy? Why, Thummy, Thummy? Why, Thummy, Thummy—*Why?*'

Thumb.

'That you may drink, little finger, when you are dry?'

But this ditty did not bring out the snake. I remarked this to the old man, who replied: 'He hasn't made his toilet yet— hasn't rubbed his scales up, sir; but he'll be here presently. You will see. Keep your eye on that hole, sir. I am now going to give him a livelier tune, which is a great favourite of his'; and forthwith he struck up an old song, beginning:

"'Twas in the merry month of May,
When bees from flower to flower did hum.'

Out came the snake before the song was half over! Before it was concluded he had crawled slowly and (if I dare use such a word) rather majestically, to within a few paces of the spot where the old man was standing.

'Good morning to you, sir,' said the old man to the snake. 'I am happy to see you in your new suit of clothes. I have picked up your old suit, and I have got it in my pocket, and a very nice pair of slippers my old wife will make out of it. The last pair that she made of your rejected apparel were given as a present to Colonel Cureton, who, like myself, very much resembled the great General Blücher in personal appearance. Who will get the pair of which I have now the makings, Heaven only knows. Perhaps old Brigadier White, who has also a Blücher cut about him. What song would you like next? 'Kathleen Mavourneen?' Yes, I know that is a pet song of yours; and you shall have it.'

The old man sung the melody with a tenderness and feeling which quite charmed me, as well as the snake, who coiled himself up and remained perfectly still. Little reason as I had to doubt the truth of any of the old man's statements, I certainly should have been sceptical as to the story of the snake if I had not witnessed the scene I have attempted to describe.

'Well, sir,' said the old man, coming up to me, after he had made a salaam to the snake and left him, 'it is almost breakfast-time, and I will, with your permission, bid you good morning.'

I thanked him very much for his information, and suffered him to depart; and then, alone, I wandered about that well-filled piece of ground. I have always had a melancholy pleasure in strolling from tombstone to tombstone, and reading the various epitaphs, and on that morning, after all that I had heard from the old pensioner, I was just in the humour for gratifying this morbid desire.

~

Some miles to the northward of Meerut is the station of Burnampore. No troops are quartered here; it is what is called in India a purely civil station, containing only a magistrate (who is also the collector of the revenue), an assistant (a covenanted civilian), the establishment of the office, and a small police force. To these two gentlemen and their few subordinates were entrusted the care and the collections of a district as large as Lancashire or Yorkshire, and containing, possibly, as many inhabitants. The idea of two gentlemen keeping in order a district of such dimensions was simply absurd; but they did their best, and that was all that could be expected of them. I remained four days and nights at Burnampore, and during that time was a guest of the assistant magistrate, whose acquaintance I had made at Meerut. Anything more monotonous and dreary than the existence of a gentleman stationed at such a place it would be very difficult to imagine. My host assured me that if it were not for an occasional visit paid by some traveller on his way up or down the country, both himself and his superior officer would have died of ennui. 'If it were not for the shooting, which is very good in this district,' he added, 'I would rather be a permanent passenger on board ship, or the inmate of a debtors' prison in London, or any other part of England—in either case, one would have something like company, and one would have, at all events, a somewhat cooler and more congenial climate.'

In the district of Burnampore there are a great number of wolves, and during my short stay, even, two were brought in, and the Government reward (two rupees a head) claimed upon them. These ferocious creatures often carry off the young children of poor people and devour them. It was in this district that 'a wolf child,' as the natives of India express it, was found some years ago, and taken to Meerut, where it was exhibited as a curiosity. 'There can be no question,' said my friend and host, when I spoke to him one morning on this subject, 'that the male wolf, in all these cases, seizes and runs off with the infant, and that when he has carried it alive to the den, the female, especially if she happens to have cubs at the time, instead of killing and devouring, suckles and fosters the little human being. So, after all, the story of Romulus and Remus may not be a mere fable.'

'No,' said I. 'But what is that Greek epigram from the Anthology of Bland and Merivale? The she-goat that suckled the whelp of a wolf, which wolf, when she had no more milk to give it, killed her and eat her. Something about:

'Be kind, be gentle, and do what you will,
A stubborn nature will be nature still.'

'Yes,' replied my host. 'I do remember something about it; and by and bye we will talk the matter over, and refer to the volume, which I have amongst my books; but at present you must excuse me, for I have a duty to perform. You may come with me and witness the operation, if you like; but understand me, I shall not be offended if you decline to do so.'

'What operation?'

'That of hanging.'

'What? Hanging! Hanging what?'

'A man—a culprit—a murderer. Is is a part of my duty to see this operation performed. Come,' he added energetically, and slapping me on the shoulder. 'Come, be a sort of Selwyn for once in your life.'

Whilst I was hesitating, the magistrate approached in his buggy. He had been taking his morning drive, and had dropt in upon his assistant to have some friendly conversation. He had forgotten all about the forthcoming execution; and, on hearing that we were just about to start for the spot, he very kindly offered to take us there—an offer which was accepted by his assistant with many thanks. So, off we drove, three in a gig, like so many men going to witness a pugilistic encounter in England during the beginning of the present century.

When we had arrived at the place of execution, a field some distance from the gaol, in which had been erected a temporary gallows, I was surprised at not finding a mob. There was no one there but the culprit—who was eating as much rice as he could, and as fast as he could—a couple of native policemen with drawn swords guarding him; the gaoler, who was a Mahommedan, and a Bengalee writer (clerk), who stood with pen, ink, and paper in hand, ready to dot down the official particulars of the scene, preparatory to their being forwarded to Government, according to a certain regulation.

'Is everything ready?' said the assistant magistrate to the gaoler.

'Yes, Sahib,' he replied; 'but he has not yet finished his breakfast.'

'In one minute, Sahib,' cried the culprit, who overheard the conversation; and hastily taking into his stomach the few grains of rice that remained upon the dish, and drinking the remainder of his half-gallon of milk, he sprang up, and called out the word 'Tyear!' signifying 'I am ready.' He was then led up to the scaffold, the most primitive affair that I ever beheld. It was only a piece of woodwork resembling a large crock or crate in which a dinner-service is packed for exportation.

Upon this crock, which was placed under the beam, he was requested to stand. Having obeyed this order, the rope was adjusted around his neck. The assistant magistrate then called out to him in Hindostanee, 'Have you anything to say?'

'Yes, Sahib,' was the reply. And he began a long story, false from beginning to end, but every word of which the Bengalee writer took down. He spoke, and with vehemence, for about thirty-five minutes, when, having stopped, either finally, or to take breath, the assistant magistrate gave the signal to the gaoler, by waving his hand. The crock was then pulled from under the culprit by the two policemen, and down dangled the culprit's body, the feet not more than eighteen inches from the ground.

They are not adepts in the art of hanging in India; it took the culprit at least ten minutes to die.

At times I feared, so desperate were his struggles, that he would break the beam, snap the rope, or bring down the whole apparatus. In the days of Henry Fielding, the vulgar used to speak of hanging as 'dancing on nothing,' and this horrible idea the Indian culprit on that morning amply realised. The reader must not, however, sympathize with his sufferings. He had been justly convicted, and was justly put to death for murdering, in that very field where he expiated his offence, a little girl of seven years of age, in order to possess himself of a single bangle she wore—a bangle valued at one rupee four annas—half-a-crown of English money. I cannot accuse myself of a cruel or brutal disposition; but, if the monster whom I saw hanged had had a thousand lives instead of one, I could have witnessed the taking of every one of them without a single atom of a desire to save him.

The cutting down of the culprit, as soon as it was discovered that life was extinct (for as there was no crowd of pickpockets and vendors of cakes and ginger-beer to take a moral lesson, the prescribed hour was unnecessary) was quite as primitive as the foregoing part of the operation. One of the native policemen with his blunt sword, severed the rope by sawing it just above the tie, and down came the corpse. I was tempted to jump out of the buggy in which, sitting between the magistrate and his assistant, I had witnessed the execution, and examine, or rather look attentively at, the deceased. A finer head, in a phrenological point of view, I had never seen, and across the naked chest was suspended the sacred thread, indicating that the culprit was a Brahmin.

'Is it not very odd,' said I, on my return to the buggy, 'that most of the diabolical crimes committed in this country are committed by Brahmins?'

'Not at all odd,' replied my host. 'Do you not know that they believe nothing can hurt their pure souls after death; and hence their comparative recklessness in this world? There was a Brahmin hanged here, about a year ago, who, just before he was turned off, made a speech such as that made by Napoleon on paper to Sir Hudson Lowe—'You may convict me of what you please; you may make me a prisoner; you may, if you like, shackle these limbs, and consign me to a dungeon; but you will find that my soul will be just as free, just as proud, as when it awed all Europe!'

'Ah, but that was the emanation of ——'

'What the deuce is that?' cried the magistrate, who was driving us rapidly towards home. 'See! That thing in the road.' And coming up to it, he reined in the horse.

The syce (groom), who was running behind the buggy, picked up the object, at his master's bidding. It was a cloak—a lady's cloak—made of most costly materials—satin and silk, and wadded throughout. It had evidently fallen, unobserved, from some palanquin during the night, and an examination of the footprints showed that the last traveller who had moved along the road was journeying upward, and was then most probably staying at the dâk bungalow, at Deobund, a halting-place some twelve miles distant. The assistant magistrate, after we had breakfasted, proposed that he and I should drive to Deobund, and make inquiries. I was nothing loth, and a swift mare having been harnessed and put to the buggy, off we started, two sowars (native horsemen or mounted police) cantering behind us.

About two miles from the bungalow to which we were proceeding, we overtook a tribe of large monkeys. I should say there were as many as four hundred, and each carried a stick of uniform length and shape. They, moved along in ranks or companies, just, in short, as though they were imitating a wing of a regiment of infantry. At the head of this tribe was an old and very powerful monkey, who was no doubt the chief. It was a very odd sight, and I became greatly interested in the movements of the creatures. There could be no question that they had either some business or some pleasure on hand, and the fact of each carrying a stick led us to conclude that it was the former upon which they were bent. Their destination was, like ours, evidently Deobund, where there are some hundreds of monkeys fed by a number of Brahmins, who live near a Hindoo temple there, and perform religious ceremonies. They (this monkey regiment) would not get out of the road on our account, nor disturb themselves in any way, and my friend was afraid to drive through their ranks, or over any of them, for when assailed they are most ferocious brutes, and armed as they were, and in such numbers, they could have annihilated us with the greatest ease. There was no help for us, therefore, but to let the mare proceed at a walk in the rear of the tribe, the members of which, now that we were nearing Deobund, began to chatter frightfully. Just before we came to the bungalow, they left the road, and took the direction of the temple. Fain would we have followed them; but to do so in the buggy would have been impossible, for they crossed over some very rough ground and two ditches. My friend, therefore, requested the sowars to follow them, and report all they might observe of their actions. Meanwhile we moved off to the bungalow, in search of the owner of the cloak. The first person whom we saw was an ayah, who was sitting in the verandah, playing with a child of about five years of age.

'Whose child is that?' asked the assistant-magistrate of the ayah.

'The mem-Sahib's.'

'What is the mem's name?'

'I don't know,' she replied, with a smile which seemed to say that she was not warranted in being communicative. While travelling, few servants who know their business will tell strangers the name of their master or mistress.

'What is *your* name?' he then inquired of the boy, in English.

'I don't understand you,' was the reply, in Hindostanee, accompanied by a shake of the head. It is wonderful how rapidly the children of Europeans in India take a cue from a native servant of either sex. Not always, but in very many cases, it is in deceit and falsehood that children are first schooled by the servants. The reader must understand that deceit and falsehood are not regarded as immoralities in the eyes of Asiatics. A man or woman who, by fraud and perjury wins a cause, or gains any other point, is not looked down upon as a rogue, but up to as a very clever fellow. Several other experiments were made in order to extract from the ayah the name of her mistress, but to no purpose. The only information we could learn was, that the lady was much fatigued, and was sleeping. We said nothing about the cloak, by the way.

The servants of the bungalow, and at Deobund (there were four of them) now came up to make their most respectful salaam to one of the lords of the district, the assistant-magistrate, on questioning them in private as to the name of the lady, we were in no way successful. All that the ayah would tell them, they said, was, that she had come from Calcutta, and was going to Simlah. 'She is a burra beebee, however, Sahib,' added the Khansamah; 'for all along the road, after she left the steamer at Allahabad, until she arrived at Meerut, she was escorted by two sowars; and when she reaches the Saharunpore bungalow, she will find sowars ready. This is the only district in which she has had no escort.'

This was a mystery that my friend could not unravel: why, if other magistrates had been indented upon (as magistrates very frequently were, when ladies were nervous and travelling with only an ayah), he should be omitted; especially as his district was as dangerous to pass through as any other (not that there was much or any danger in those days), was more than he could understand; and he very naturally became all the more curious (apart from the ownership of the cloak) to know the name of the lady who had broken the link of her escort when she came into his district. 'Perhaps,' said he to me, 'either I have or my chief has given her husband some offence, and, possibly, he is small-minded enough to decline asking me to do what after all is only a matter of duty, or of civility and compliment, which amounts to pretty much the same thing. However, we shall see.'

My friend now mentioned to the Khansamah, a very old but very active and intelligent man, the sight we had seen on the road—the regiment of monkeys.

'Ah!' exclaimed the old man, 'it is about the time.'

'What time?'

'Well, Sahib, about every five years that tribe comes up the country to pay a visit to this place; and another tribe comes about the same time from the up-country—the hills. They meet in a jungle behind the old Hindoo temple, and there embrace each other as though they were human beings and old friends who had been parted for a length of time. I have seen in that jungle as many as four or five thousand. The Brahmins say that one large tribe comes all the way from Ajmere, and another from the southern side of the country, and from Nepal and Tirhoot. There were hundreds of monkeys here this morning, but now I do not see one. I suppose they have gone to welcome their friends.'

The sowars who had been deputed to follow the tribe now rode up, and reported that in the vicinity of the old temple there was an army of apes—an army of forty thousand! One of the sowars, in the true spirit of Oriental exaggeration, expressed himself to the effect that it would be easier to count the hairs of one's head than the number there assembled.

'Let us go and look at them,' I suggested, 'and by the time we return the lady may be stirring.'

'But we will not go on foot,' said my friend; 'we will ride the sowars' horses. In the first place, I have an instinctive horror of apes, and should like to have the means of getting away from them speedily, if they became too familiar or offensive. In the second place, I do not wish to fatigue myself by taking so long a walk in the heat of the day.'

We mounted the horses, and were soon at the spot indicated by the sowars. There were not so many as had been represented; but I am speaking very far within bounds when I state that there could not have been fewer than eight thousand, and some of them of an enormous size. I could scarcely have believed that there were so many monkeys in the world if I had not visited Benares, and heard of the tribes at Gibraltar. Their sticks, which were thrown together in a heap, formed a very large stack of wood.

'What is this?' my friend said to one of the Brahmins; for since his appointment he had never heard of this gathering of apes.

'It is a festival of theirs, Sahib,' was the reply. 'Just as Hindoos at stated times go to Hurdwar, Hajipore, and other places, so do these monkeys come to this holy place.'

'And how long do they stay?'

'Two or three days; then they go away to their homes in different parts of the country; then attend to their business for four or five years; then come again and do festival, and so on, sir, to the end of all time. You see that very tall monkey there, with two smaller ones on either side of him?'

'Yes.'

'Well, sir, that is a very old monkey. His age is more than twenty years, I think. I first saw him fifteen years ago. He was then full-grown. His native place is Meerut. He lives with the Brahmins at the Soorj Khan, near Meerut. The smaller ones are his sons, sir. They have never been here before; and you see he is showing them all about the place, like a very good father.'

Having seen enough of these 'sacred animals,' we returned to the bungalow; we were only just in time, for the lady was about to depart, albeit the sun was very high in the heavens, and the day, for the time of year, was extremely hot. We caught sight of her in the verandah. My friend became deadly pale, and exclaimed: 'Is it possible!'

'What?' I asked him.

'I will tell you on our way home. I must see her—speak to her—painful as our meeting must be. Only fancy, if that cloak should be hers!'

The lady, who must have learnt from the servants at the bungalow the name of my friend, the official, evidently desired to avoid an interview with him; for upon our approach she retired from the palanquin, which she was arranging, and entered hastily the room she had occupied. We (my friend and myself) went into the other room of the bungalow, which happened to be vacant. Presently we heard the voice of the ayah. She was very angry and was accusing the servants of the bungalow of being thieves. She had now, for the first time since they were lost, missed several articles, and amongst them the cloak of her mistress. She was perfectly ready to swear that she had seen them all since their arrival at the bungalow; that she had removed them from the palkees with her own hands; and if the servants had not stolen them who had?—who could have done so? Distinctly did we hear the lady command the ayah to be silent—to say nothing of the loss, and enter her palanquin; but the ayah, too much enraged to hear or to heed the command, repeated her accusation; whereupon the servants in a body rushed into the apartment in which we were standing listening, and after protesting their perfect innocence of the theft, referred to the character for honesty which every one of them had borne for many years. Strange to say, frequent as are the opportunities which the servants at these bungalows have of pilfering from travellers, they rarely or never avail themselves of such opportunities; and, whenever it has happened that a lady or gentleman has died in one of them, the money and effects have always been forthcoming, with nothing whatever missing.

The lady now forced the ayah to depart, and enter her palanquin, in which the little boy was sitting; she was about to follow, when my friend rushed into the verandah, and, seizing her by the hand, detained her. She was as agitated as he was; and quite as pale. He held her hand in his with a firm but withal a gentle grasp, and looked into her face, which must have been beautiful when she was a few years younger. As it was, she had still a charming profile and countenance, and a skin as white as snow. From the window, or rather looking through the Venetians, I beheld the scene, which reminded me of that exquisite picture of Mr. Frank Stone—*The Last Appeal*. There was a look of agony and despair in the face of the man; while the woman, who appeared to sympathise with his sufferings, did not for awhile raise her eyes from the ground. But at length she did so, and, looking mournfully into my friend's face for a few seconds, burst into tears, and presently her head, involuntarily as it were, rested on his shoulder. Suddenly recollecting herself, she again attempted to take her departure; but my friend, now grown desperate seemingly, placed her arm beneath his, and walked with her to a clump of shade-giving mango trees, in front of the bungalow, and there they held a conversation which lasted some ten minutes. The lady then tore herself away from my friend, and after bidding him farewell, she threw herself into her palanquin, which was speedily lifted by the bearers and borne away, followed by the two sowars, who were commanded to escort the fair traveller to the next station. My friend, from the verandah of the bungalow, watched the procession till it was out of sight, and then, seating himself on the steps, covered his face with his hands, and wept like a child.

'Come!' I said, after a time, laying a hand on his shoulder.

'I am not very impatient to know your secret, but it is time that we thought of returning. What about the cloak? You have not restored it to the owner.'

'No, my dear fellow, and I never intend to do so. She has consented to my retaining it. That cloak has warmed her dear limbs, and the sight of it shall warm my heart till the last hour of my existence.'

On the way home my friend (who was accidentally drowned in the river Jumna, about two years ago) spoke as follows:

'Ten years have now elapsed since that lady and I were fellow-passengers on board of a ship bound from London to Calcutta. She was then seventeen years of age, and I twenty. On the voyage we became very much attached to each other, and eventually loved each other devotedly. And, what was more, we were betrothed. It was arranged that as soon as practicable we should be married, I was compelled, on arrival, to remain at the college at Fort William for a year, to pass an examination; she was obliged to proceed to a large station in Bengal, to join her family. Her father was a member of the civil service; previous to her arrival he had promised Alice (that is her name) to an old man, a judge, who had been twice married, and who was then a widower. This old man was very rich, and had—as he still has—a great influence with the government. A brother of his was one of the lords of Leadenhall-street, and of this country. For some time after our unhappy separation we corresponded regularly; but suddenly the correspondence ceased. Her letters to me, and mine to her, were intercepted. Meanwhile, the old judge, to whom she had been promised, paid his addresses to her. She refused him. Many devices were resorted to in order to wean her affections from me. They all failed. At length they hit upon one which had the desired effect. They caused a paragraph to be inserted in one of the Calcutta journals, to the effect that I had married the daughter of a half-caste merchant. Alice was permitted to see this paper, but none of those containing my indignant denial of the truth of the announcement.

'In disgust at my imagined faithlessness, and in despair and recklessness, Alice at length accepted the hand of the old judge. They were married. When made acquainted with this horrible fact, I became half-mad. I drank very hard, had an attack of *delirium tremens*, and was sent home for change of air and scene, to recruit my health. On my return to India, after an absence of eighteen months, I was sent to Dacca, where there was not the slightest chance of my ever seeing Alice. Subsequently, I was, at my own request, transferred to these provinces, but sent to Banda—a sort of penal settlement for refractory civilians; not that I ever committed any offence beyond that of loving Alice and being beloved by her. You must understand that, owing to the influence of his brother, her old husband, shortly after his marriage with Alice, became the great man he now is; and he had only to express a wish in this country, touching the appointment or *dis*appointment of any junior in the service, to have such wish instantly realised. My only surprise is, that when it became necessary for her to pass through this district, I was not ordered away to Scinde, on some trumpery business, alleged to be special.

Had there been any idea that we should meet—as by the merest chance we have met—again in this world, I should certainly have been removed, and ordered to some other station miles away. I have never seen her since we parted in Calcutta, now more than nine years ago, until this very day. But, thank Heaven! she loves me still!'

'I was afraid, when I saw you talking to her beneath that clump of trees, that——' I was about to make some observations.

'Ah, no!' he interrupted me. 'There is no danger. Great and lasting as my love for her is, I could not bear the thought of taking the slightest advantage of her feelings; or to see her fall from the sphere in which she holds a lofty and proud position. She is not happy, neither am I. But spirits will recognise each other, and be united for ever and ever. Ours is not a solitary case; sometimes when ladies in India fall they deserve far more of pity than of blame.'